W9-BCP-907

The
WONDERFUL
NAMES
of our
WONDERFUL
LORD

ENDURING VOICES

The WONDERFUL NAMES *of our* WONDERFUL LORD

THE CLASSIC 365-DAY DEVOTIONAL

Charles Hurlburt
T. C. Horton

BARBOUR BOOKS
An Imprint of Barbour Publishing, Inc.

Editorial Note

This book contains the complete, unabridged text of *The Wonderful Names of Our Wonderful Lord*. No changes have been made to the text, including T. C. Horton and Charles Hurlburt's style, capitalization, and spelling of words such as "Saviour." Punctuation has been lightly updated so as to conform to modern style.

© 2019 by Barbour Publishing, Inc.

Print ISBN 978-1-64352-152-7

eBook Editions:
Adobe Digital Edition (.epub) 978-1-64352-354-5
Kindle and MobiPocket Edition (.prc) 978-1-64352-355-2

Published by Barbour Books, an imprint of Barbour Publishing, Inc., 1810 Barbour Drive, Uhrichsville, Ohio 44683, www.barbourbooks.com

Our mission is to inspire the world with the life-changing message of the Bible.

Member of the
Evangelical Christian
Publishers Association

Printed in the United States of America.

1. THE SEED OF THE WOMAN

*And I will put enmity between thee and the woman,
and between thy seed and her seed.*

GENESIS 3:15

"Because He stooped so low God hath exalted Him very high" (Philippians 2:9, Arthur Way's Translation). From this first great act and fact in His revelation to that last greater act when He died for our sins on Calvary, and up until the very time when God exalted Him very high to sit at His own right hand in the heavenlies, our Saviour's example was one of profound humility. He came from the bosom of the Father to become the "SEED OF THE WOMAN." He turned from "the words which I have spoken to you, the same shall judge you," to be in His innocence judged of sinful men and crucified.

*Oh, Thou who didst humble Thyself to be born
of a woman, who didst bear our sins in Thine
own body on the tree, we bow on our faces before
Thee and worship and adore. Amen.*

---

2. THE ANGEL OF JEHOVAH

*And the angel of the LORD called unto
Abraham out of heaven the second time.*

GENESIS 22:15

The Angel (or Messenger) of Jehovah was Himself God's message to us.

Oh, Thou who dost Thyself bring Thine own Message to heal our deep desolations—Thou art our sin offering. We praise Thee for the glory which Thou givest in our pain by Thine own radiant presence and worship Thee, Oh "Angel of Jehovah." Amen.

---

3. SHILOH (PEACEMAKER)

The sceptre shall not depart from Judah, nor a lawgiver from between his feet, until Shiloh come; and unto him shall the gathering of the people be.

GENESIS 49:10

Israel must walk in darkness under law, until the years may seem eternity, but "SHILOH" comes at last and peace. Has SHILOH come to thee? And has the peace which passeth understanding, the peace He made, entered into thy soul? For Shiloh came and conquered every foe that could harass thee, and stands today offering the peace He made "that passeth knowledge." Hast thou received it? Has SHILOH come in vain for thee? Begin today and "in everything by prayer and supplication make thy requests known to him," and Shiloh's peace shall "keep thy heart."

---

4. THE STONE OF ISRAEL

But his bow abode in strength, and the arms of his hands were made strong by the hands of the mighty God of Jacob; (from thence is the shepherd, the stone of Israel).

GENESIS 49:24

Oh STONE OF ISRAEL, chief Cornerstone, rejected by the builders, Stone of Stumbling, Rock of Offense, Foundation Stone, on which alone we build aught that shall stand, make me a POLISHED, LIVING stone; built in with other stones; perchance a pillar to go out no more, but always a part of Thy temple, for Thine own indwelling. Thrice Holy Lord, self-offered for my peace; through death that I might live, through fire that I might become indestructible; consumed that I might feed on Thee in holiest communion—enlighten me today till I perceive Thy peace that passeth understanding. Amen.

---

5. MANNA

*And the house of Israel called
the name thereof Manna.*
EXODUS 16:31

There is an art, not known to all who travel, by which a wearied and exhausted life may gather, in a way which seems to those who do not understand almost miraculous, new strength, new vigor, new physical power, for an onward march. So does the Master feed the souls of His children Himself a spiritual "Manna" as real and more wonderful than that strange, mysterious food with which He fed the House of Israel. To "feed upon the Lord" may sound like empty mysticism but may be a fact to every trusting soul. For unto us are given "exceeding great and precious promises, that by Him we might be partakers of the Divine nature."

6. THE MEAT (MEAL) OFFERING

And when any will offer a meat offering unto the LORD,
his offering shall be of fine flour; and he shall pour
oil upon it, and put frankincense thereon.
LEVITICUS 2:1

Perfect communion with our God as shown in the MEAT OFFERING was in many senses the highest pattern which our Saviour set for men. Shall we not make it the chiefest plan of every day to have a time when we enter into such worship with Him that we may truly say, "There is nothing between Thee and me, dear Lord," and then carry the sweetness of that deep communion unmarred and uninterrupted through all the hours.

Most Holy Meal Offering, El Elyon, as Thou didst pour
upon the fine meal of Thy perfect life the Holy Oil of
Thy most Holy Spirit, and the frankincense of Thy perfect
Adoration, and offer all for me, so I, accepting Thine which
only hallows mine, pour forth my soul, my blood-cleansed
soul, in worship. Holy! Holy! Holy! is the Lord. Amen.

---

7. THE PEACE OFFERING

And if his oblation be a sacrifice of peace offering. . .
he shall offer it without blemish before the LORD.
LEVITICUS 3:1

Is there any point of dispute between thy Lord and thee? One little thing which thou dost not surrender? He is right. He cannot change. It is thy heart which must surrender. Then canst thou receive the peace which passeth knowledge. He has made the offering which atones for all thy past, but thou must yield thy will to Him. Shall it be now?

---

8. A STAR

I shall see him, but not now: I shall behold him,
but not nigh: there shall come a Star out of Jacob,
and a Sceptre shall rise out of Israel, and shall smite the
corners of Moab, and destroy all the children of Sheth.
NUMBERS 24:17

What could be more beautiful or more fitting than that our Lord should be called of God "A STAR"? Those who know Him best may say, "I shall see Him, but not now. I shall behold Him, but not nigh." From far beyond our world of trouble and care and change, He shines with undimmed light, a radiant, guiding STAR to all who will follow Him—a morning STAR, promise of a better day.

---

9. A SCEPTRE

A Sceptre shall rise out of Israel.
NUMBERS 24:17

There is a view of Jesus which men are slow to see, but some day all the world shall know that "A SCEPTRE" shall rise out of Israel, and evil will be destroyed before His righteousness more swiftly than ice must melt before the glowing sun. It is in the very nature of things that sin must be consumed before His glorious holiness. Can it be other than the love of sin that blinds the eyes of men to His consuming righteousness?

"Search me, O God, and know my heart. Try me and know my thoughts, and see if there be any wicked way in me and lead me in the way everlasting." Amen.

---

10. THE CAPTAIN OF THE HOST OF THE LORD

And he said, Nay; but as captain of the host of the LORD am I now come.
JOSHUA 5:14

The hosts of Israel stand before the gateway to a promised land. No swords are drawn, no skill have they, but with them is an unseen host, and with the host, "THE CAPTAIN OF JEHOVAH'S HOST." Jericho and all the giants of the land submit, and for thee, "behind the dim unknown standeth God within the shadows, keeping watch above His own."

Captain of the Hosts of God, In the path where Thou hast trod, Bows my soul in humble awe—Take command. Thy word is law. Cause me to possess the land, Led by Thine Almighty hand. Be my guide, defense and power, Lead me from this very hour. Amen.

11. THE ROCK OF MY SALVATION

The LORD liveth; and blessed be my rock;
and exalted be the God of the rock of my salvation.

2 SAMUEL 22:47

No graver danger threatens the believer than that of forgetting that he was redeemed—forgetting even in the joy of realized life what our salvation cost, and what is the rock foundation of our faith. To meet this need our Saviour pictures Himself not merely as the Rock of Ages, and our Strong Rock of Refuge, but the *Rock of our Salvation*. Here, in Him and upon His merit and atoning grace, we were saved from among the lost. Let us glory in this precious name and never forget that He was "wounded for our transgressions" and "that he bore our sins in his own body on the tree."

---

12. THE LIGHT OF THE MORNING

And he shall be as the light of the morning, when the
sun riseth, even a morning without clouds.

2 SAMUEL 23:4

No single name nor picture of our Lord could possibly reveal Him as the full supply of all our need. Our Lord is to His people not only "THE MORNING STAR" but when the lights of night shall fade in dawning day, He becomes the "LIGHT OF THE MORNING." When all of earth has passed, when all earth's visions fade and flee away, when the great glory of that morning of our eternal life in Heaven shall break upon us, we shall find that He who lighted all our earthly pilgrimage is still our source of life and guidance over there and will be to those for whom He has prepared a place, the "LIGHT OF THE MORNING." "So shall we be forever with the Lord."

---

13. TENDER GRASS

And he shall be. . .as the tender grass springing
out of the earth by clear shining after rain.
2 SAMUEL 23:4

Sheep thrive best in pastures so low and short that other animals are not able to eat it. The good Shepherd leads His flock in pastures where the "tender grass," springing up from the earth after the rain, brings to them all-sufficient nourishment as they feed on Him. Oh, ye who are partakers of the Divine nature, open now the Book of books, and humbly kneeling feed on Him who is the Living Word, "THE TENDER GRASS," which satisfies and builds up His hungry sheep.

---

14. THE DAYSMAN

Neither is there any daysman betwixt us,
that might lay his hand upon us both.
JOB 9:33

When the day of reckoning comes, when by all justice I should hear the sentence which my sins deserve, when I shall stand before the Father, stripped of all pretense and sham, then will I fear no evil, for my "DAYSMAN,"

Mediator, Arbitrator, will stand and speak for me. Can I do less than bow upon my face and worship Him, now, and throughout eternity?

---

15. MY GLORY

But thou, O Lord, art a shield for me;
my glory, and the lifter up of mine head.
PSALM 3:3

That God is "glory"—or "excellence"—beyond our understanding, none can deny. But do our hearts look up to Him today in humble, earnest worship, and know the truth, and speak the truth—"Thou art my GLORY"? Our *safety* lies in the fact that He possesses us. Our deepest, holiest *joy* comes only when we humbly say in the hour of secret worship, "Thou art mine."

Oh, Lord my Glory, be Thou my shield this day. Amen.

---

16. THE LIFTER UP OF MINE HEAD

But thou, O Lord, art a shield for me;
my glory, and the lifter up of mine head.
PSALM 3:3

Oh, Thou who hast given
Thy glory to me,
Anoint my blind eyes
Till Thy glory I see.

Lift up my bowed head,
Be my shield and my light,
Till Thy radiant glory
Shall banish my night.

---

17. FORTRESS

The LORD is my rock, and my fortress, and my deliverer;
my God, my strength, in whom I will trust; my buckler,
and the horn of my salvation, and my high tower.
PSALM 18:2

"A mighty fortress is my God," and no evil may reach the soul that shelters there. There is no saint of God who may look back through all the troubled years of any earthly pilgrimage, and not say, if he shall truly speak, "I have been kept by the power of God." Every failure of our lives and each defeat has come when we have sought some earthly fortress rather than our Lord.

I am hiding, Lord, in Thee. Amen.

---

18. A WORM AND NO MAN

But I am a worm, and no man; a reproach
of men, and despised of the people.
PSALM 22:6

Few harder experiences come to God's children than in these days when those who should be friendly, unjustly make us a reproach, and when they say in the midst of trials which are not the result of any sin in us, "Aha, Aha," as though they themselves are righteous, when perchance their sin has brought to us the pain—yet *He* has walked that way before us. He, too, was "A REPROACH OF MEN"! Shall not the servant walk there too, and be like Him who in such suffering "opened not His mouth"?

Lord Jesus, who didst bear scorn and reproach for me,
give me the grace of true humility. Amen.

---

19. MY SHEPHERD

The LORD is my shepherd; I shall not want.
PSALM 23:1

To say, "The Lord is MY SHEPHERD," must carry with it in our understanding not merely grateful praise for the infinite grace and tenderness of the Great Shepherd who leads us by still waters and in green pastures, but confession of our own helplessness and need of a Shepherd's care. And a remembrance also of our lost, undone condition, until

> "All through the mountains, thunder-riven,
>   And up from the rocky steep,
> There arose a glad cry to the gates of Heaven,
>   'Rejoice! I have found My sheep!' "

Lord Jesus, Thou tender Shepherd, lead us
forth this day in glad service for Thee. Amen.

20. RESTORER

He restoreth my soul: he leadeth me in the
paths of righteousness for his name's sake.
PSALM 23:3

We wander from God and from the paths of righteousness—from following Him beside the still waters—till we lose the way, lose joy, lose the sound of His voice. Then the Master "restoreth [the only use of this form in the Old Testament] our soul"; "brings us back into His way," into the paths of righteousness.

Oh, gracious "RESTORER," bring back my wandering
soul as a straying sheep, and lead me on in the paths
of righteousness "for Thy name's sake." Amen.

---

21. THE STRONG AND MIGHTY JEHOVAH

Who is the King of glory? Jehovah strong
and mighty, Jehovah mighty in battle.
PSALM 24:8 ASV

Is thy heart faint? Thy strength but utter weakness? Behold thy LORD—Jehovah—"He who reveals Himself" as "STRONG AND MIGHTY"—a soldier, a warrior, with sufficient power to break down every opposition. Hear Him say, "My presence shall go with thee to conquer every foe."

Strong and mighty Jehovah, give me victory over
all the power of the enemy this day. Amen.

22. JEHOVAH, MIGHTY IN BATTLE

Who is the King of glory? . . . Jehovah mighty in battle.
PSALM 24:8 ASV

No life can be lived for God in these difficult days without terrific conflict. Foes within and foes without assail each saint continuously. Principalities and powers are arrayed against the child of God who seeks to serve his Master. We have no might with which to meet "this great host that cometh out against us," but Jehovah, Mighty in Battle, is our Saviour, our Intercessor, our Elder Brother, our ever-present Friend.

*"Sure, I must fight if I would win;
increase my courage, Lord." Amen.*

---

23. KING OF GLORY

*Who is this King of glory? The LORD of hosts,
he is the King of glory.*
PSALM 24:10

Jehovah Jesus, the glorious King! Not merely a king, but glorious, excelling all others in mighty truth and power, grace and love. We almost forget for a time His absolute sovereignty as we bow in humble worship before His matchless glory and cry again and again,

"Thy Kingdom come," Oh, Glorious King. Amen.

24. MY STRONG ROCK

Bow down thine ear to me; deliver me speedily;
be thou my strong rock, for an house of defence to save me.
PSALM 31:2

No sorrow of men is so deep and dark and bitter as to be without a refuge, a rock, a safe retreat. My soul, however deep thy sorrow, however dark thy sin, however hopeless thy lot among men, the Man of Sorrows bore thy sin in His own body on the tree. He carried all thy grief. He is thy "STRONG ROCK." A strong, safe house, in which I am defended from myself, the world, the devil.

"Rock of ages, cleft for me,
Let me hide myself in Thee."
Amen.

---

25. MY ROCK AND MY FORTRESS

For thou art my rock and my fortress; therefore
for thy name's sake lead me, and guide me.
PSALM 31:3

Some day our work shall all be tried by storm and by fire and the question will be of our foundation. Are we built upon the Rock of Ages, that High Rock which is a Fortress, so that, though the wind blows and the storm shakes all about us, we shall stand secure? And if Christ be our "ROCK" and our "FORTRESS" shall we build with "wood and hay and stubble" upon such an eternal foundation?

Lord Jesus, may we seek to gather "gold and silver and precious stones," that we may bring some honor to Thee, our "ROCK AND FORTRESS," by building that which shall endure through all the ages. Amen.

---

26. THE ROCK THAT IS HIGHER THAN I

From the end of the earth will I cry unto thee, when my heart is overwhelmed: lead me to the rock that is higher than I.
PSALM 61.2

Not down to a dungeon deep,
    Nor to level of earth, hard by—
But lead, when the storm o'erwhelms,
    To "the ROCK that is HIGHER THAN I."

Up from my sin's dark slime,
    Away from the world's mad cry—
To Thee do I come, O Christ!
    To "the ROCK that is HIGHER THAN I."

There will I worship and wait
    Redeemed, with the saints on high.
All glory, and honor, and praise
    To "the ROCK that is HIGHER THAN I."

27. A STRONG TOWER

For thou hast been a shelter for me,
and a strong tower from the enemy.
PSALM 61:3

What is the testimony of *our* souls today as we read that
which others have said concerning Him who has been a
"STRONG TOWER" from the enemy? Did ever a child of
God in danger hasten within the Strong Tower of His
Presence and find aught of failure or defeat? Must we not
confess that every failure has come when we were found
outside?

Oh, Thou Strong Tower, may we enter
in today and dwell in Thee and be safe.

---

28. A STRANGER AND AN ALIEN

I am become a stranger unto my brethren,
and an alien unto my mother's children.
PSALM 69:8

What was the price He paid,
That, what He bore for me;
"A STRANGER, AN ALIEN";
alone, He died on Calvary.

A "STRANGER" to make me a friend,
An "alien" to give me a home.
Great Stranger, I fall at Thy feet,
No longer from Thee will I roam.
Amen.

29. THE KING'S SON

Give the king thy judgments, O God,
and thy righteousness unto the king's son.
PSALM 72:1

How little do our hearts discern the homage due to God as KING and to Jesus as His SON. We bow our heads, we lift our hats, we pay our homage to the fleeting, trifling power of earth's great men, but do we, as we enter the house of God, bow humbly and revere THE KING'S SON? Are earthly thoughts hushed and earthly words stilled as we gather in the house of God, and even when our spokesman voices our desires to Him, do wandering thoughts of earthly things deprive us of the blessing and the answer to our prayers?

Lord, teach us how to pray, that
we may truly worship Thee. Amen.

---

30. RAIN UPON MOWN GRASS

He shall come down like
rain upon the mown grass.
PSALM 72:6

My soul was parched with the fire of sin,
My life mowed down with pain,
My Saviour spoke, "My child, draw near."
His word was like THE RAIN.

Refreshing, cleansing, lifting me,
My Lord, my All, came down,
And now I turn from all earth's dross—
To gain a Heavenly crown.

---

31. SHOWERS UPON THE EARTH

He shall come down like rain upon the mown grass:
as showers that water the earth.
PSALM 72:6

Our lives grow dusty, dry and desert in our earthly
pilgrimage, but He who seeks a love that is fresh and
pure and strong comes down upon us as "THE SHOWERS
UPON THE EARTH." Have you turned to Him today and
found that cool, refreshing, cleansing blessing which He
seeks to give?

> *"There shall be showers of blessing,*
> *Oh, that today they might fall!*
> Now, *as to God we're confessing,*
> Now, *as on Jesus we call."*
> *Amen.*

---

32. MY FIRST-BORN

Also I will make him my firstborn,
higher than the kings of the earth.
PSALM 89:27

"Loose thy shoes from off thy feet, for the place where
thou standest is holy." The Eternal Father, God, is

speaking. "My First-born I will make higher than the kings of earth." Oh, thou who art the last-born of the Father, the First-born is thy Elder Brother. Thou hast shared His humiliation to thy salvation. Thou shalt share His exaltation to thine eternal glory.

We worship Thee; Lord Jesus, God's "First-born"! *Amen.*

---

33. THE HEAD STONE OF THE CORNER

The stone which the builders refused
is become the head stone of the corner.
Psalm 118:22

Men may reject "*The Head Stone of the Corner*" and seek to erect a building that shall stand, without the Living Christ. But God has laid aside all human plans and made our Lord and Saviour "The Head Stone of the Corner." When all human buildings crumble and every man-taught architect has failed, all hearts bow before that perfect building, that eternal temple, worshipping Him who is its crown of grace.

---

34. MY HIGH TOWER

My goodness, and my fortress; my high tower, and my
deliverer; my shield, and he in whom I trust; who subdueth
my people under me.
Psalm 144:2

"My High Tower" is a vision of our glorious Saviour as the Most High—high above our trials; high above our temptations; high above our foes; high above our failures and losses; high above the fret and care of our earthward life. A place of holy calm and peace and stillness. The door is open.

Lord Jesus, our High Tower, let us enter in today. Amen.

---

35. WISDOM

I wisdom dwell with prudence,
and find out knowledge of witty inventions.
PROVERBS 8:12

Wisdom is the right use of knowledge. What a wondrous name for Him who gave Himself for us! Who, "when He putteth forth His own sheep goeth before them"; who guides us by the skillfulness of His hand.

May we seek with all our hearts until we find Thee, and finding Thee, find WISDOM to do the will of God. Amen.

---

36. EXCELLENT

Let them praise the name of the LORD:
for his name alone is excellent.
PSALM 148:13

"All the glory of the Lord is that in which He excels all others." "HIS NAME IS EXCELLENT," and all His names which represent some feature of His grace are glorious because they excel any other name ever uttered among men. What friend, what helper do we know on earth that ever has or can approach His excellence? And so we turn with new deep joy to the Psalmist's testimony, "They that know Thy name shall put their trust in Thee."

37. UNDERSTANDING

Counsel is mine, and sound wisdom;
I am understanding; I have strength.
PROVERBS 8:14

God is Love, God is Light, God is to us a thousand things for which we long and which we need, but have we realized that in possessing Him and abiding in Him, He is "UNDERSTANDING" and all that seems dark and difficult will become clear to us as we depend upon Him, who is "UNDERSTANDING"? It would take ten thousand years to learn a few of the many things we long to know on earth. The soul that is linked to God begins to understand and will go on to clearer understanding throughout the countless ages.

38. A FRIEND THAT STICKETH CLOSER THAN A BROTHER

A man that hath friends must shew himself friendly:
and there is a friend that sticketh closer than a brother.
PROVERBS 18:24

Stay, lonely pilgrim, searching long for fellowship. Stop here and find "A FRIEND." "There is a Friend," though all the world deny it. One who is always true and faithful. One who never leaves and ne'er forsakes. No brother will, or can, abide as He. Will you be friend to Jesus, as He is friend to thee?

We worship Thee, we trust all to Thee, and take from Thee all peace, all grace, all needed power to do and be what pleaseth Thee, our never-absent FRIEND. Amen.

39. OINTMENT POURED FORTH

Because of the savour of thy good ointments thy name is as ointment poured forth.
SONG OF SOLOMON 1:3

Is thy soul sore from sin, from chafing, or from the fiery darts of Satan, of sinners, or of saints? Then is thy Lord to thee as "OINTMENT POURED FORTH," free, abundant, ready, healing, and fragrant. Suffering soul, come near to Him and let that healing OINTMENT pour over thee and soothe and heal thee.

40. BUNDLE OF MYRRH

A bundle of myrrh is my well-beloved unto me.
SONG OF SOLOMON 1:13

Oh, Child of Sorrow, Church of Smyrna, sad soul suffocating in earth's dark vapors, thy Lord is for thee an exquisite perfume, "A Bundle of Myrrh." A missionary, wearily walking a winding pathway in the night, suddenly came upon a spot where the air was heavy with the perfume of wild jasmine, and was comforted and refreshed by a fragrance preserved from nonappreciative wild animals and wilder men for a sorrowing toiler. So is thy Lord, to thee, "A Bundle of Myrrh."

---

41. CLUSTER OF CAMPHIRE

My beloved is unto me as a cluster of camphire in the vineyards of Engedi.
Song of Solomon 1:14

A beautiful, fragrant flower—"a cluster" of them— exquisite beauty, exquisite perfume in abundance! Struggling in the midst of experiences that are not fragrant, that are not delightful, hast thou learned to turn to Him, who, in the midst of darkness, is Light, in the midst of battle, is Peace, in the midst of unpleasantness, is to thee unlimited and exquisite delight? Dost thou know thy Lord as "A Cluster of Camphire"? Acquaint now thyself with Him, and be at peace.

---

42. THE ROSE OF SHARON

I am the rose of Sharon.
Song of Solomon 2:1

Child of God, there is no mood of thy life where Jesus fails to fit thy need; to brighten as a brilliant rose thy life.

In joy or sorrow, sunshine or shadow, day or night, He blooms for thee. Behold Him, then, today, not only on the Cross for thee, not only on the Throne, but near thee, close beside thy path, "THE ROSE OF SHARON."

---

43. THE LILY OF THE VALLEYS

I am. . .the lily of the valleys.
SONG OF SOLOMON 2:1

Sweetest, fairest, most exquisite flower that eye hath seen hidden save to eyes that seek it out. So does thy Lord unveil Himself to thee, even though thou walkest through the valleys. Only in those deeper shadows canst thou know His utter loveliness. Behold *Him* then, and "fear no evil."

---

44. HIM WHOM MY SOUL LOVETH

I will rise now, and go about the city in the streets, and in the broad ways I will seek him whom my soul loveth.
SONG OF SOLOMON 3:2

Not in the doubting throng,
Not in the boastful song,
But kneeling—with Christ above me—
Humbly I'll say, "I love Thee."

Not with my lips alone,
Not for Thy gifts I own,
But just for the grace I see
Jesus, my soul loveth Thee. *Amen.*

45. THE CHIEFEST AMONG TEN THOUSAND

My beloved is white and ruddy,
the chiefest among ten thousand.
SONG OF SOLOMON 5:10

Do we sometimes sing with too little depth of meaning "He's the Chiefest of Ten Thousand to my soul"? Is He really first in our hearts' affection? If so, His presence has been real to us for He has said, "Ye shall seek Me and ye shall find Me, when ye search for Me with all your heart," or, "with your whole desire." Here the secret of full transforming communion with our Lord Jesus Christ is found in gazing upon Him in all the beauty of His holiness, until in very truth He becomes in our hearts the "CHIEFEST OF TEN THOUSAND."

---

46. ALTOGETHER LOVELY

His mouth is most sweet: yea, he is altogether lovely.
SONG OF SOLOMON 5:16

Every earthly joy will pall,
Every earthly friend will fall.
Only Christ is to the end
"ALTOGETHER LOVELY," Friend.

Do you see His wondrous face?
Full of glory, love and grace?
Look, and all thy need confess,
Worship His pure Holiness.

47. THE BRANCH OF THE LORD

*In that day shall the branch of the
LORD be beautiful and glorious.*
ISAIAH 4:2

By every means and picture which we can understand
the Spirit reveals our Saviour's oneness with God. None
is more clear or full of meaning to us than this, "THE
BRANCH OF THE LORD." One with the Father, growing
out of and yet a part of Him. And we are "branches" of
Christ. (See John 15.) As we worship the Christ who is
very God, we hear Him say, "If ye abide in Me, ye *shall
ask what ye will, and it shall be done unto you.*"

---

48. JEHOVAH OF HOSTS

*And one cried unto another, and said, Holy, holy, holy,
is Jehovah of hosts: the whole earth is full of his glory.*
ISAIAH 6:3 ASV

The "Jehovah" of the Old Testament is the "Jesus" of the
New. If we always think (as Scofield suggested) of
Jehovah as "God revealing Himself," and the words of
Jehovah—Jesus, "Blessed are the pure in heart for they
shall see God," then shall the heavens about us be always
full of the chariots and horsemen of Jehovah of Hosts,
and all fear shall be stilled and His revelation of Himself
to us will not be in vain.

*Lord Jesus, Jehovah of hosts, give us a
vision of Thy glory this day. Amen.*

49. THE CHILD

*For before the child shall know to refuse the evil,
and choose the good, the land that thou abhorrest
shall be forsaken of both her kings.*

ISAIAH 7:16

The first, last, and chiefest mark of Christ's Deity was
His great humility. The greatest Sage and Seer of all
the ages, "A CHILD"! The Everlasting God, hoary-white
with eternal years, "A CHILD"! Then shall *we* hesitate to
"become as little children" knowing that only so shall we
enter the kingdom?

---

50. A SANCTUARY

And he shall be for a sanctuary.

ISAIAH 8:14

Where is thy place of worship? Where, in the turmoil
of the street; where, in the busy cares of home; where,
in the hurry and confusion of men, shall our souls find
the place to pray? "He shall be for a 'SANCTUARY,' closer
to thee than breathing, nearer than hands or feet." At
any moment during all the hurried day thou mayest be
hidden from all earth's eyes, and still from all earth's din.
Only abide in Him.

51. A GREAT LIGHT

*The people that walked in darkness have seen a great
light: they that dwell in the land of the shadow
of death, upon them hath the light shined.*

ISAIAH 9:2

It is the people who once walked in darkness who are
able to see the greatness of the light. It is the soul which
finds that it is lost that seeks the Lord. Have *you* seen the
Light? The beloved apostle said, "That which we have
seen, declare we unto you, and this is the message that
we declare unto you that God is Light, and in Him is no
darkness."

*Lord, let my life and lips tell out the story
of the LIGHT my eyes have seen. Amen.*

---

52. WONDERFUL

*For unto us a child is born, unto us a son is given. . .
and his name shall be called Wonderful.*

ISAIAH 9:6

Jesus is "the same yesterday, today, and forever," and
men who think Him commonplace or at most only
an unusual man, will some-time stand ashamed and
confounded as they hear this prophecy fulfilled, "His
name shall be called WONDERFUL." Today He is working
just as wonderful works as when He created the Heaven
and the earth. His wondrous grace, His wonderful
omnipotence, is for His child who needs Him and who

trusts Him, even today. Attempt great things for God and expect great things from Him, and you will begin even now to say, His name is WONDERFUL.

---

53. COUNSELLOR

*For unto us a child is born. . .and his
name shall be called. . .Counsellor.*
ISAIAH 9:6

Not often is He called "COUNSELLOR" now. Even God's saints continuously ask of men instead of God, "How may I find God's will?" Conference after conference is held by both the world and the church to find by human wisdom some better plan for earthly government, or for the church, or for the welfare of our earthly life and walk. But how rarely do we bow together or alone to seek that Heavenly wisdom, that Divine counsel, which alone will enable us to find our way out of the mazes in which we wander. When shall His Name be joyfully and triumphantly proclaimed as "Counsellor" by His people? By thee?

---

54. THE MIGHTY GOD

*For unto us a child is born, unto us a son is given. . .
and his name shall be called. . .The mighty God.*
ISAIAH 9:6

Have we doubted His might and feared, in the day when some foe was near? Hark! His name is "The Mighty God." Then away with all doubt and fear! "Thou hast made both the Heaven and earth. There is nothing too hard for Thee."

Lord, I bow to the dust and worship.
Mighty God, show Thy power in me! Amen.

---

55. THE EVERLASTING FATHER

For unto us a child is born, unto us a son is given. . .
and his name shall be called. . .The everlasting Father.
ISAIAH 9:6

Who has not mourned a father's death and felt the loss of his transient power and helpfulness? The Child who was born in Bethlehem, who gave His life for thee, is not alone thy Saviour and thy King, but "His name shall be called *the Everlasting Father*." In His everlasting love, within His everlasting arms, within His Father-heart which pitieth thee—His child, thou shalt find safety, rest, and comfort.

---

56. THE PRINCE OF PEACE

For unto us a child is born, unto us a son is given. . .
and his name shall be called. . .The Prince of Peace.
ISAIAH 9:6

He who proclaimed to loyal hearts, "My peace I leave with you. My peace I give unto you. Not as the world giveth give I unto you," is rightly called "THE PRINCE OF PEACE." He who brought such peace to earth was rejected of men, and waits still to be crowned on earth; but He gives before that royal day a peace that passeth understanding to every trusting heart. Have you received it? Will you, in loyalty to "the Prince of Peace," accept in humble faith His peace today?

---

57. THE LIGHT OF ISRAEL

And the light of Israel shall be for a fire, and his Holy One for a flame: and it shall burn and devour his thorns and his briers in one day.
ISAIAH 10:17

Jesus was and is the "LIGHT OF ISRAEL." He is also the "Light of Life" and the "Light of men," a "Light to lighten the world." But the "Light of Israel" was "to burn and devour thorns and briers." Dear child of God, are you bringing the useless branches, the unpleasant, unlovely things of your life into the Light of His Presence that they may be consumed? Some day the shining of His Presence will destroy the very Advocate of evil. Shall we not submit our lives to that Wondrous Light and ask Him to consume all evil in us?

58. A ROD OUT OF THE STEM OF JESSE

And there shall come forth a rod out of the stem of Jesse,
and a Branch shall grow out of his roots.

ISAIAH 11:1

Only a "rod" from a human "stem"? Only a "root" from "dry ground"? Hath He no "form nor comeliness," no "beauty that we should desire"? "Surely He bore our griefs" and the way of "our peace" was in Him. "Because He stooped so low God hath exalted Him very high," and the comeliness of a tender plant was the glory of God on high.

---

59. A BRANCH OUT OF HIS ROOTS

And a Branch shall grow out of his roots.

ISAIAH 11:1

Of all the miracles that attest to the Deity of our Lord, including the miraculous preservation of the Scriptures, none is more wonderful or convincing to the honest, faithful heart than the preservation, not only of Israel, but of that section of Israel, humble in its origin, which revealed our Lord to be born of the family of David and of Jesse. Out of the nations scattered over the earth, out of the line of kings who long had ceased to reign, there came forth, as the prophet said, a "BRANCH OUT OF THE ROOTS" of the stem of Jesse. And He who was of the seed of David shall just as surely come again to reign once more over Israel, and through Israel over all the earth.

Lord, our faint hearts believe anew in God's
eternal truth and faithfulness. Amen.

---

60. THE ROOT OF JESSE

And in that day there shall be a root of Jesse. . .to it
shall the Gentiles seek: and his rest shall be glorious.
ISAIAH 11:10

It is not Israel alone who shall rejoice when "a root of
Jesse shall stand for an ensign of the people," for "to it
shall the Gentiles seek," and all the gracious promises
and gifts God gave to Jesse and to David and his seed
which could bring rest and comfort to our souls belong
to us who worship Jesus, David's Son, and Jesse's Root.
How all the grace and glory of our God through all the
ages, is gathered up for us who from the Gentile world
bow at His feet and find His glorious rest!

---

61. THE ENSIGN OF THE PEOPLE

And in that day there shall be a root of Jesse, which shall
stand for an ensign of the people; to it shall the Gentiles
seek: and his rest shall be glorious.
ISAIAH 11:10

Jesus is the people's flag, an "ENSIGN OF THE PEOPLE."
Wherever and whenever He is lifted up the people seek
after Him. Is not our failure to win many to the Lord
due to our misrepresentation of Him? To our failure to
reveal the beauty of His holiness and to enter into His

glorious rest? Shall we bow in humble confession while we pray that we who are His representatives may be saved from misrepresentation of Him by lives that are cruelly unlike Him and seek for grace to exalt Him everywhere among men?

---

62. MY STRENGTH AND MY SONG

Behold, God is my salvation; I will trust, and not be afraid: for the LORD JEHOVAH is my strength and my song; he also is become my salvation.

ISAIAH 12:2

We know Jehovah is our "STRENGTH" but do we make Him also our "SONG"? As we make Him so and sing of Him, we lose our fear. We are able to "trust and not be afraid," only as we *sing* of Him. Our Redeemer *is* our "*strength*." Make Him your "SONG" today.

---

63. A NAIL FASTENED IN A SURE PLACE

And I will fasten him as a nail in a sure place; and he shall be for a glorious throne to his father's house.

ISAIAH 22:23

Men have dreamed fantastic ideas concerning Christ as a "*Nail in a Sure Place.*" Whatever else this name may or may not mean, it brings to the worshipping child of God a sense of the fixedness, the certainty and security of Jesus Christ in His relationship to the temple and throne of God. If we on earth are being builded together for an habitation of God, yet more sure is the fact of the presence of Christ filling the house. If we are "pillars who go no more out," it is because He is secure—His place is "fastened" and "sure." "So shall we be ever with the Lord," for where He is, there shall also His servant be, and our abiding is as sure as Christ's.

---

64. A GLORIOUS THRONE TO HIS FATHER'S HOUSE

And he shall be for a glorious
throne to his father's house.
ISAIAH 22:23

One of the most vivid pictures painted by the Holy Spirit of the life that lies beyond follows in The Revelation—the swift, wondrous vision of the church on earth (Revelation 4:2–3). "Behold, a throne was set in Heaven. . .and there was a rainbow round about the throne." That rainbow brings us hope and comfort and the precious, glorious promise that our Lord Himself is a "GLORIOUS THRONE TO HIS FATHER'S HOUSE." Let it be no longer hard or difficult for thee to pray. The throne before which you bow is not one of austere justice but rather one of infinite grace. Let us therefore come boldly to the THRONE OF GRACE, that we may obtain mercy and find help.

65. STRENGTH TO THE POOR AND NEEDY

For thou hast been a strength to the poor,
a strength to the needy in his distress.

ISAIAH 25:4

Touched with the feeling of our infirmities our Lord in His omnipotence becomes a "Strength to the Poor and Needy." Let us never forget that His strength is made perfect in our weakness only when we realize our helplessness and fling ourselves, as trusting children, into the outstretched arms by which He "created the heavens and the earth." With what a wondrous picture does our Lord reveal Himself as the supply for our every need and "strength to the poor"!

---

66. A SHADOW FROM THE HEAT

For thou hast been. . .a shadow from the heat.

ISAIAH 25:4

In the intolerable heat of the sun as it beats upon the plateaus of equatorial Africa, one may step from the unbearable heat to a shade so cool, so refreshing, that until it is experienced it is almost beyond conception or belief. Thus our Lord pictures Himself to His weary, toiling children, struggling onward in the heat of almost impossible experiences, as a *Shadow from the Heat,* into whose presence we may step at any moment of our pilgrimage and find cool, refreshing rest.

67. A REFUGE FROM THE STORM

For thou hast been. . .a refuge from the storm. . .when the
blast of the terrible ones is as a storm against the wall.
ISAIAH 25:4

"God is faithful who will not suffer you to be tempted above that ye are able, but will, with every temptation, make a way of escape," a "refuge from the storm," "that ye may be able to bear it." It needs must be that we pass through storms and that we feel their force and chilling blast, for only in such experiences could we ever know the comfort, the witness, of Him who is our *"Refuge from the Storm."* Are we hiding in Him?

---

68. THE ROCK OF AGES

Trust ye in Jehovah for ever; for in Jehovah, even Jehovah,
is an everlasting rock. (Margin, "a rock of ages.")
ISAIAH 26:4 ASV

Many of the college buildings at Oxford University, hundreds of years old, were described by one who studied there more than half a century ago as "leprous with age." Many are crumbling away, and some must be replaced to save the buildings. The strongest rocks in which men hide the bodies of departed friends are ofttimes riven by a growing plant. But He who calls us to "trust in Jehovah forever" calls Himself *"An Everlasting Rock"* or *"The Rock of Ages."* Let us trust in Him today, tomorrow, and forever.

69. A CROWN OF GLORY

In that day shall the Lord of hosts be for a crown
of glory. . .unto the residue of his people.
ISAIAH 28:5

We hear and think much of redeemed and fruitful saints shining as stars in the diadem of our Lord, but in this wondrous title of our glorious Saviour we have a new vision of His relationship to His people. Souls who have been down-trodden and scorned by those whom the world calls great, will in that day as He honors redeemed believers as His Bride, find that the presence, the tender and gracious love of the King of Glory, will be to them in the eyes of all, a witness, a CROWN OF GLORY. Oh, thou who art redeemed from among the lost, thou who wast dead and art alive, wast lost and art found, behold His wondrous grace! The King of kings, the Lord of lords, shall be to thee a CROWN OF GLORY. Then fall at His feet today and worship Him with all thy heart.

---

70. A DIADEM OF BEAUTY

In that day shall the Lord of hosts be for. . .
a diadem of beauty, unto the residue of his people.
ISAIAH 28:5

The difference between a Crown of Glory and a Diadem of Beauty is that in the first the excellence, the worth, the value, the glory of God shall be upon the saints. While in the other, the beauty, the very radiance of the Lord, shall fill and shine out from those who, in a moment, in the twinkling of an eye, shall be changed into His likeness. O, humble child of God, behold the exceeding grace which shall be revealed in the ages to come. The beauty of the Lord our God shall be upon thee, and He shall be to thee a crown or DIADEM OF BEAUTY. "He that hath this hope in Him purifieth himself."

71. THE FOUNDATION

Therefore thus saith the Lord GOD, Behold,
I lay in Zion for a foundation a stone.
ISAIAH 28:16

Of all the gracious promises concerning the children of God none is more wonderful than that which describes the saints as polished stones in the temple where He dwells. With Divine grace our Lord calls Himself "THE FOUNDATION," an "Everlasting Rock," "The Rock of Ages." Where stands our faith today? Are we building upon the sands of human philosophies, or upon Him?

"On the Rock of Ages founded,
Naught can shake our sure repose."

72. A SURE FOUNDATION

Therefore thus saith the Lord GOD,
Behold, I lay in Zion. . .a sure foundation.
ISAIAH 28:16

All the chiseling, all the polishing of experiences through which we pass, is costly. Will it last? Is it worthwhile?

Worthwhile to suffer on and say, "Dear Lord, stay not Thine hand to comfort us and steady us." Through just such testing times the Master calls Himself a "SURE FOUNDATION." No experiment here, no doubt, no room for anxious thought or fear. He who builds upon that "*Sure Foundation*" finds his building sure, and he shall be a "pillar in the temple of God," to "go no more out forever."

---

73. A TRIED STONE

Therefore thus saith the Lord GOD, Behold,
I lay in Zion for a foundation a stone,
a tried stone, a precious corner stone.
ISAIAH 28:16

How strange is this experience of our Lord. Surely the Father knew the Son, knew His every capacity and power. Yet He was tried of God as we have need to be tried, only that He might leave us an "example that we might walk in His steps." What mockery, what hopeless blasphemy, that He should be rejected by some builders! Let us bid the great Master Builder to try us and to chisel us until we fit in the place which He has prepared for us.

---

74. A COVERT FROM THE TEMPEST

And a man shall be as. . .a covert from the tempest.
ISAIAH 32:2

Of no other being could such language be used, in no other literature of the world is such marvellous imagery to be found, as that used in the Word of God to picture the grace and glory of our Lord. When the destructive tempests sweep and we hide in Him, shall we be safe? He shall be a "*Covert from the Tempest*"—covered, sheltered, safe. Are we hiding in Him?

---

75. AS AN HIDING PLACE FROM THE WIND

And a man shall be as an
hiding place from the wind.
Isaiah 32:2

Standing one day on the deck of a steamer in the harbor at Aden, a traveler saw a storm of wind sweeping across the desert like some high, mountainous wave, rolling and sweeping forward until it struck the sea and lashed it to foam. Then on across the bay until it struck the ships lying there at anchor, till nearly every boat was torn from its moorings or forced to loosen every cable and steam with full force into the face of the terrific wind. No hiding place was there. So do the storms of hate, of evil, and of sin sweep over our lives as we journey toward our everlasting home. But for every soul who knows his own helplessness, our Saviour is Himself a "Hiding Place from the Wind."

76. SHADOW OF A GREAT ROCK IN A WEARY LAND

And a man shall be as. . .the shadow
of a great rock in a weary land.
ISAIAH 32:2

Journeying one night in the wilderness of central Africa in a section plagued by many ravenous beasts, we found no place of safety till we came to the shadow of a great rock, where we sat down with our backs to the rock and, building at our feet a great fire, found rest and refreshing for the next day's still weary journey. O weary child, when thy strength fails and thou canst go no further, sit down and lean back in the shadow of thy Lord, upon Him. Build there in prayer the fire of faith and find rest and refreshment for thine onward march.

---

77. AS RIVERS OF WATER IN A DRY PLACE

And a man shall be as. . .
rivers of water in a dry place.
ISAIAH 32:2

To know the blessing of water in abundance we need to have felt a very keen thirst. Wandering one time in part of Africa's desert, two missionaries traveled without water until thirst became first a pain, then an agony, then almost insanity. After long marching over dry, burning sands they came to the waters of a wide, deep river and quenched their thirst. "If any man thirst let him come unto Me," and He is near. No matter how deep our thirst, how great our longing or our need, He who is as *"Rivers of Water in a Dry Place"* has said, "Lo, I am with you. Drink, and be satisfied."

78. THE KING IN HIS BEAUTY

Thine eyes shall see the king in his beauty;
they shall behold the land that is very far off.
ISAIAH 33:17

"Blessed are the pure in heart, for they shall see God." Do our lives see the King in His beauty? Do we grip the fact that as we gaze upon Him it is His will that we should be changed unto the same likeness, "from glory unto glory"? "A little while and the world seeth Me no more, but YE SEE ME." No more wonderful promise is ours for present experiences than this. O Lord, let every mist and veil that hide Thy glory be removed, and every sin be put away, that we may behold Thee in the beauty of holiness. Then "the beauty of the Lord thy God shall be upon thee."

79. OUR LAWGIVER

For the LORD is our judge, the LORD is our lawgiver,
the LORD is our king; he will save us.
ISAIAH 33:22

Every nation, every act, every life, needs a law to direct it in its relation to its own expression, and to others. That law must be made by one who knows and understands the nation, act, or life. Jesus is our "LAWGIVER." He who gave us life, He who has lived the life we need to live—He knows. He made the law for us in infinite tenderness and love. "He that hath My commandments and keepeth them, He it is that loveth Me."

---

80. JEHOVAH

The voice of one that crieth, Prepare ye in the wilderness the way of Jehovah; make level in the desert a highway for our God.
ISAIAH 40:3 ASV

Jehovah—"The Self-existent One who reveals Himself." Into the wilderness of my lost way He comes to find me and lead me out. Into the desert of my barren life enters Jehovah and makes all the desert a garden. Into my death He brings His life and to my dead senses reveals Himself The One Eternal God. Shall we not bow before His Majesty and worship Jehovah, while we pray for greater grace to receive all the revelation of Himself which He would give?

---

81. THE LORD JEHOVAH

Behold, the Lord Jehovah will come as a mighty one, and his arm will rule for him: Behold, his reward is with him, and his recompense before him.
ISAIAH 40:10 ASV

Not every soul that worships Jehovah has learned that the secret of all power and of fullness of blessing is in making Him the Master of our lives. Adonai Jehovah is the Lord, the Ruler, the Master, who in eternal grace reveals Himself. Shall we not humbly bow at His feet and crown Him Lord, Master, of all that we have and are?

---

82. THE EVERLASTING GOD

Hast thou not known? Hast thou not heard,
that the everlasting God, the LORD, the Creator
of the ends of the earth, fainteth not, neither is
weary? There is no searching of his understanding.
ISAIAH 40:28

Everlasting, never-ending,
    Age-abiding is my Lord.
Never shadow caused by turning,
    Changeless, perfect, is His Word.

Everlasting God, I pray Thee
    Steady, strengthen, stablish me.
Safe from grief and pain and failure,
    Hide me, Everlasting God, in Thee.

---

83. A LIGHT OF THE GENTILES

I the LORD have called thee in righteousness,
and will. . .give thee. . .for a light of the Gentiles.
ISAIAH 42:6

"In Him was life, and the life was the Light of men." But how shall that Light lighten the Gentiles unless we who are the light of the world shall go forth among the Gentiles and let the light shine? Someone brought that Light to us. Shall we not bear it on a little farther into the darkness of some other life? He *is* the Light. He *gave* the Light. *We* are the *Light-bearers*.

---

84. MINE ELECT

Behold my servant, whom I uphold; mine elect,
in whom my soul delighteth; I have put my spirit upon
him: he shall bring forth judgment to the Gentiles.

Isaiah 42:1

Infinite God, who knows and understands, the God of wisdom and of knowledge, called in review all angels and all men of all the ages and of all time and chose our Lord and called Him "Mine Elect," to be the world's Redeemer, Saviour, Friend and the believer's All in All. Does thy choice fall on Him, each day, each hour, in each experience? May He be all in all to thee today.

---

85. THE POLISHED SHAFT

And he hath made my mouth like a sharp sword;
in the shadow of his hand hath he hid me,
and made me a polished shaft.

Isaiah 49:2

In every part of the Word of God our Lord is pictured as the "Word of God" having a "voice as the sound of many waters," and speaking to His people words of peace and comfort and of power. But no name of Christ is more true of Him than that He is a "*Polished Shaft*," and when He speaks and His word cuts through our selfish lives like a sword of radiant light, let us rejoice. The Adversary of our souls would make us proud of self. Few human friends are faithful, but He who is "A Polished Shaft" speaks not only with eternal love but with unchanging faithfulness.

"Speak, Lord, for thy servant heareth thee." Amen.

---

86. THE HOLY ONE OF ISRAEL

Thus saith the LORD, the Redeemer of Israel, and his Holy One, to him whom man despiseth, to him whom the nation abhorreth, to a servant of rulers, Kings shall see and arise, princes also shall worship, because of the LORD that is faithful, and the Holy One of Israel, and he shall choose thee.
ISAIAH 49:7

All Israel walked in sin. All Israel was defiled. And yet in cloud by day, in fire by night, within the Holy tabernacle there stood a Presence, Holy, Infinite in love and grace and power. "*The Holy One of Israel*" could not forget His chosen people nor resist their faintest cry. So Israel stood and lived, and lives today because "THE HOLY ONE OF ISRAEL" stood beside them. And beside thy soul He stands today to be thy righteousness and lead thee to Himself. Behold Him, and adore!

87. A ROOT OUT OF A DRY GROUND

*For he shall grow up before him as a tender
plant, and as a root out of a dry ground.*
ISAIAH 53:2

Dear discouraged soul, does it seem sometimes to thee
that thy lot is a hard one? That thou hast been asked to
stand in difficult places and where surrounding conditions have been most unfavorable? He who redeemed
thee knows every difficulty, every sorrow, which thou
canst feel. Dishonored by ignorant doubters, He must
needs turn even to the wondrous mother who had
received both natural and supernatural knowledge of His
Divine character and mission and ask, "How is it that
ye sought me? Wist ye not. . . ?" He hath suffered "in all
points like as we" and is, therefore, "able to succor" us.
Then "consider Him who grew up a ROOT OUT OF A DRY
GROUND," lest ye grow weary and faint in your minds.

---

88. A MAN OF SORROWS

*He is despised and rejected of men; a man of sorrows,
and acquainted with grief: and we hid as it were our faces
from him; he was despised, and we esteemed him not.*
ISAIAH 53:3

He who was the source of all joy, the giver of all peace,
He before whom angels and archangels bow in adoration,
is also called a Man of Sorrows. Grief broke His heart,
crushed out His life. Shall we through disobedience,
rebellion, or lack of love or service, or worship, add to

the sorrows which He bore, or shall we murmur if we too shall be permitted to partake of His sorrows, or to share His grief? He sorrowed all alone, save perhaps as angels ministered to Him in Gethsemane's deep shadow. But He shares thy grief, He carries all thy sorrow and comforts those who trust in Him. Shall we not worship and adore the *Man of Sorrows*?

---

89. MY RIGHTEOUS SERVANT

He shall see of the travail of his soul, and shall be satisfied: by his knowledge shall my righteous servant justify many; for he shall bear their iniquities.

ISAIAH 53:11

There are many servants, only *One* is righteous. Paul was able to say, "I have declared unto you the whole counsel of God, I have fought a good fight, I have kept the faith," but still must call himself an unprofitable servant, and less than the least of all saints. Shall we therefore become discouraged and conclude that it is not worthwhile to try? Nay, "your labor is not in vain in the Lord," for He who was "MY RIGHTEOUS SERVANT" shall justify many." For He is still "Jehovah Tsidkenu" (our Righteousness), and we may bring the dropped stitches of our best weaving, and the broken efforts of our best service, and laying all at His feet rejoice that we are justified by Him who is God's "Righteous Servant."

90. MY MAKER

For thy Maker is thine husband.
Isaiah 54:5

We hear of "self-made men," of men who are made by their surroundings, or by devoted friends and fellows. How rarely do we hear today the humble, joyful boast, "By the grace of God I am what I am." And yet "He is thy Maker"! All thou art that is lasting, all thou art that is good, all thou art that is helpful, God has made. Bow then before thy Maker. Worship and petition Him to finish that which He began.

---

91. THE GOD OF THE WHOLE EARTH

For. . .the Lord of hosts is his name; and thy Redeemer the Holy One of Israel; The God of the whole earth shall he be called.
Isaiah 54:5

Is there any part of the earth that is mine? Not till I am truly a child of "The God of the Whole Earth." May I not receive Him and possess all things in Christ and proceed to enjoy them, untroubled by the world's woe? Not till the whole earth has heard that He is "The God," not of a few, but "of the whole earth."

92. A WITNESS TO THE PEOPLE

Behold, I have given him for a witness to the people,
a leader and commander to the people.

Isaiah 55:4

A witness of the love of God, the grace, the power, the holiness of Deity. No flaw in all that matchless testimony, no doubtful, double-meaning speech, and He could say, "He that hath seen me hath seen the Father." We too are Witnesses, but oh, how full of flaws is all our testimony! The Father dwelt with Him, and He sought the Father's guidance at every step and every word. We too may see and hear and walk with God, and so alone shall our witness win the wanderers home.

---

93. A LEADER

Behold, I have given him for. . .
a leader and commander to the people.

Isaiah 55:4

From the beginning of our Christian lives the fact that "He leadeth me" is one of the most blessed thoughts that comes to a child of God. But we think most often of His leading to battle, leading out of the mazes of confusion and ignorance, leading through the darkness of our night. Do we realize that infinite tenderness that makes Him gently lead those who are doing the finest and the most difficult and unknown service of the world? The sorrow, the loneliness, the pain, which no friend on earth can know, He understands, He feels with us, and gently leads us through the shadows to His own great glory. Shall we not follow where He leads, and keep so close to Him that we shall never miss the way?

---

94. A COMMANDER

Behold, I have given him for a. . .
commander to the people.
ISAIAH 55:4

In a day when nearly every man desires to do that which is right in his own eyes, it becomes difficult for all God's children to recognize His right to command. Yet He who redeemed us, who bought us so that we are not our own, proclaimed His right to the title of "COMMANDER." Failure to obey will account for most of the loss of communion and joy in prayer and in the study of God's Word. If there be any commandment which He has brought home to our hearts which we have not obeyed, shall we not today grant Him instant, cheerful, loving obedience, and make Him in every detail of life our COMMANDER?

---

95. THE REDEEMER

And the Redeemer shall come to Zion, and unto them
that turn from transgression in Jacob, saith the LORD.
ISAIAH 59:20

When failure comes and disappointment, when thy soul has been defeated and the race seems hopeless, stop and think "thy Lord redeemed thee and at countless cost." If He saw in thee that for which to pay His life, Himself, His all, is it not worthwhile to rise and try again, walking with Him and worshipping Him who redeemed thee?

---

96. THINE EVERLASTING LIGHT

Thy sun shall no more go down; neither shall thy moon withdraw itself: for the LORD shall be thine everlasting light, and the days of thy mourning shall be ended.
ISAIAH 60:20

No picture is more difficult for us to spiritually apprehend than a time when the sun shall no more go down. When Christ shall be to us "EVERLASTING LIGHT." Our lives are so filled with ups and downs, with lights and shadows, that stability seems almost inconceivable, and everlasting darkness easier to understand than everlasting light. Yet such is Christ to thee. Then enter in with holy boldness and walk in EVERLASTING LIGHT.

---

97. THE ANGEL OF HIS PRESENCE

In all their affliction he was afflicted, and the angel of his presence saved them: in his love and in his pity he redeemed them; and he bare them, and carried them all the days of old.
ISAIAH 63:9

A nervous, restless boy, in his early childhood, called out again and again in the night, "Daddy, are you there?"

The father answered, "Yes, I am here. Do you want anything?" "No, I only wanted to be sure you were there." And the frightened boy, still in the dark, went directly to sleep. Oh, child of God, beset by fears and troubled so that thou hast found no rest, let "THE ANGEL OF HIS PRESENCE" comfort thee. Unstop thy ears. Speak to Him, and thou shalt hear the voice of Him who spake as never man spake, saying, "Lo, I am with thee."

---

98. OUR POTTER

But now, O LORD, thou art our father; we are the clay,
and thou our potter; and we all are the work of thy hand.
ISAIAH 64:8

Have you understood the meaning of the force that presses in upon your life today? Has it seemed only pain, only wrong and deep injustice? Back of all that seems to be, the POTTER *stands*, with an ideal so lofty that our highest imagination has not fully grasped it. A beauteous, transformed life, fit to sit with Him upon His throne, is in the POTTER's mind, and He is shaping thee through that which seemed a rude experience. Shall we not learn to say today,

"I am the clay, and Thou THE POTTER.
Shape me as Thou wilt, dear Lord." Amen.

99. BALM OF GILEAD

Is there no balm in Gilead. . . ?
JEREMIAH 8:22

There are experiences of suffering through which the Master wills that we should pass. There are burdens which He does not lift, though He takes us, burden and all, into His everlasting arms. But in every suffering which He permits, He is our "BALM." He eases every pain. He comforts every sorrow. He strengthens us in every weakness. There is a "Balm" in our Gilead. Shall we take from Him the comfort which He offers us today?

---

100. MY PHYSICIAN

Is there no balm in Gilead; is there no physician there? why then is not the health of the daughter of my people recovered?
JEREMIAH 8:22

Dr. Arthur T. Pierson once said in a sermon preached in London, England, that one of the marked proofs of our failure to live up to the light we have, is found in our failure to obey the commandment in James' epistle, "Is any among you sick? Let him call for the elders of the church and pray over him." We rush at once to secure human aid, forgetting even to pray as we go, or that He who formed us and through whose blessing alone the human means can be effective, is "OUR PHYSICIAN."

101. MY PORTION

The portion of Jacob is not like them: for he is the former of all things; and Israel is the rod of his inheritance: The LORD of hosts is his name.

JEREMIAH 10:16

When we are able to lay hold of the fact that Jesus is "OUR PORTION" then do we truly possess all things, for "how shall He not with Him freely give us all things?" Nay, more, "For all things are yours. Whether Paul, or Apollos, or Cephas, or the world, or life, or death, or things present, or things to come, all are yours. And ye are Christ's and Christ is God's." Shall we seek to appropriate all of His matchless love and grace and hope and courage and joy and fruit and power? What more can we ask, or have?

---

102. THE HOPE OF ISRAEL

O the hope of Israel, the saviour thereof in time of trouble, why shouldest thou be as a stranger in the land, and as a wayfaring man that turneth aside to tarry for a night?

JEREMIAH 14:8

"The Hope of His People," Israel, is also the Hope of His Bride, the church. Israel shall be regathered and become, though now despised of man and all nations, the chiefest kingdom in all the earth. And when He shall come He shall be both "HOPE" and full fruition to every believing soul.

"Even so come, Lord Jesus, come quickly." Amen.

103. A RIGHTEOUS BRANCH

Behold, the days come, saith the LORD, that I will raise unto David a righteous Branch, and a King shall reign and prosper, and shall execute judgment and justice in the earth.

JEREMIAH 23:5

A "righteous servant" is one who serves righteously, satisfying every command of his master. A "righteous branch" is one which rightly respects, honors, and bears fruit to the tree from which it grows. "Ye are branches," our Saviour said of us, but He also said, "My Father pruneth." He who is the RIGHTEOUS BRANCH heard the Father say, "This is my beloved Son in whom I am well pleased." Shall we not seek with all our hearts to so abide in Him that we shall glorify the Father by bearing much fruit?

---

104. DAVID, THEIR KING

But they shall serve the LORD their God, and David their king, whom I will raise up unto them.

JEREMIAH 30:9

What doubt, what incredulity of men has blinded human eyes lest they should see that David, Israel's King, shall truly be raised up unto them! How much we lose of deep reality, of wondrous truth and vivid picture in the Word of God because our eyes are holden through our unbelief. How beautiful, how wonderful, that Christ our coming Lord should call Himself "DAVID, THEIR KING." What are our thoughts and prayers concerning Israel?

Are we seeking, hoping for their King and telling them that He is our King too? And praying that their eyes may be anointed to behold in Christ, "DAVID, THEIR KING"!

---

105. RESTING PLACE

My people hath been lost sheep: their shepherds have caused them to go astray, they have turned them away on the mountains: they have gone from mountain to hill, they have forgotten their restingplace.

JEREMIAH 50:6

Truly there is rest for the weary, for Jesus is "OUR RESTING PLACE." Therefore, in the midst of the toil and the weariness, in the midst of the struggle and strife, let us ask that our ears may be opened to hear Him who said, "Come unto Me, all ye who labor and are heavy laden, and I will give you rest." To abide in Him in continuous love and obedient faith is to find Him "OUR RESTING PLACE."

---

106. THE SHEPHERD OF ISRAEL

And I will set up one shepherd over them. . . and he shall be their shepherd.

EZEKIEL 34:23

Is any name more comforting to weary, needy children of our God than Jesus' name of Shepherd? Feeding, leading beside still water, watching over all our wanderings, bringing us as the Shepherd of Israel brought His flock out of the wilderness over the Jordan into the land of peace and plenty.

Teach us to trust in Thee,
O Shepherd of Israel. *Amen.*

---

107. FEEDER

And I will set up one shepherd over them, and he shall feed them, even my servant David; he shall feed them, and he shall be their shepherd.

Ezekiel 34:23

The lie of the Adversary to God's children is always that they are "lost." Or that "difficulty is a sign that God has ceased to know or care." When we have wandered from Him, from right, from rest, from peace, "He Restoreth My Soul." It is His self-appointed task—the work which love makes a necessity for Him, as well as for His wandering sheep.

"How gentle God's commands,
How kind His precepts are."

What He feeds is as important for us to learn as *when* and *where*. So let us cultivate our appetite, our longing, for His righteousness, and we shall find He is "Our Feeder."

108. A PLANT OF RENOWN

And I will raise up for them a plant of renown, and they shall be no more consumed with hunger in the land, neither bear the shame of the heathen any more.

 EZEKIEL 34:29

Although our Lord came as a tender plant, and with no form nor comeliness, yet has He become a *Plant of Renown*, for already no other name is so widely known, no other name carries such wondrous power, no other name shows such boundless grace, and sometime, perhaps soon, "every knee shall bow and every tongue proclaim" that "the Tender Plant" is a "PLANT OF RENOWN," that "Jesus Christ is Lord to the glory of God the Father."

---

109. A STONE CUT WITHOUT HANDS

Thou sawest till that a stone was cut out without hands, which smote the image upon his feet that were of iron and clay, and brake them to pieces. . . . And the stone that smote the image became a great mountain, and filled the whole earth.

DANIEL 2:34–35

Men plan for peace in human governments, build courts of arbitration, leagues of nations, pacts and pledges, only to find them crumbling in utter failure before the human work is half complete. The Eternal God is planning a kingdom and a government that cannot fail, and He the King, whose shape and form and size and power are ordered by the Most High God, will smite in His coming every man-made plan. Are we looking for that "Stone" to come and smite? Shall we be "ready in the day of His power"?

---

110. THE ANCIENT OF DAYS

I saw in the night visions, and, behold, one like the Son of man came with the clouds of heaven, and came to the Ancient of days, and they brought him near before him. . . . His dominion is an everlasting dominion, which shall not pass away, and his kingdom that which shall not be destroyed.

DANIEL 7:13–14

"In the beginning was the Word," and He who redeemed us is "THE ANCIENT OF DAYS," "whose head is white as snow" (Revelation 1:14). He was from everlasting and will be unto the ages of ages our Eternal God. Shall not we, whose life upon the earth is but a hand-breadth, bow in worship and adoration at the feet of "THE ANCIENT OF DAYS"?

---

111. THE PRINCE OF PRINCES

He shall also stand up against the Prince of princes; but he shall be broken without hand.

DANIEL 8:25

By every word which men could understand Almighty God has sought to exalt His Son, so that in all things He might have the pre-eminence in our lives, as King of kings, as Lord of lords, and as in this text, "The Prince of Princes." In earthly kingdoms it is very often true that upon the prince who is heir apparent to the throne is lavished more affection than upon the King himself. What about our love and affection to "The Prince of princes"? Although sitting now at the right hand of the Father and one with Him, He is waiting to be crowned on earth. Do we pay Him more devotion and deeper love than we do to these erring mortals who reign over us? Let us, in the real things of daily life, exalt Him to His rightful place and pour out our devotion to Him.

---

112. THE HOPE OF HIS PEOPLE

The Lord also shall roar out of Zion, and utter his voice from Jerusalem; and the heavens and the earth shall shake: but the Lord will be the hope of his people, and the strength of the children of Israel.

Joel 3:16

There is no hope apart from Him; no hope in self to win against the world, the flesh and the Devil! No hope in self to either be or do that which shall bless the world; but there is glorious hope for those who trust in Him. Jesus who is our Saviour, King and Bridegroom, the Living Head of the Body of which we are but humble members, "He is the Hope of His People." He it is that "worketh in me both to will and to do."

113. RULER

But thou, Bethlehem Ephratah, though thou be little among the thousands of Judah, yet out of thee shall he come forth unto me that is to be ruler in Israel; whose goings forth have been from of old, from everlasting.

MICAH 5:2

Never in the history of the world has there been such hopeless failure of human governments as now. Never such high ideals, and never have high ideals fallen so flat. Great plans are made and conferences held to promote peace and good government, and like flimsy houses of cards the highest hopes are shattered in ruthless, heartless, brutal war. So must it be until He who has the right to reign shall come and be "RULER," not alone in Israel, but in all the world. More than thirty years ago one who was a chosen spokesman of the Lord said, "Perhaps He would have come sooner if we had, from our hearts, prayed more earnestly 'Thy Kingdom come.' " Do we ask it and sincerely desire it?

---

114. STRONG-HOLD

The LORD is good, a strong hold in the day of trouble; and he knoweth them that trust in him.

NAHUM 1:7

During the late terrible war when the huge flying craft sailed over London, multitudes of people hid in the subways of London. In the Highlands of Central Africa there is a section known as "The Iron Stone Plateau," where the amount of ore appears to attract the lightning, and many adventurers in that section stopping long at a place, dig cellars into which they go when thunder-storms arise. There are dangerous storms which beset our spiritual life from which there is no safe retreat but Christ. Is He your "STRONG-HOLD"? Have you learned to hide in Him?

---

115. WALL OF FIRE

For I, saith the LORD, will be unto her a wall of fire round about, and will be the glory in the midst of her.
ZECHARIAH 2:5

All of defense that we need is God to those who trust in Him. A wall of fire through which the fiercest foe can never come. The foe of evil thoughts will be burned. The hasty tongue will be consumed. The selfish desire that creeps so insidiously through every other barricade will be consumed by Him who is a "WALL OF FIRE" when we shall hide in Him.

---

116. MY SERVANT, THE BRANCH

Hear now, O Joshua the high priest, thou, and thy fellows that sit before thee: for they are men wondered at: for, behold, I will bring forth my servant the BRANCH.
ZECHARIAH 3:8

No lesson, not even that of courage, is more often repeated, and perhaps none is more often needed, than the lesson given us in our Lord's humility. He upon whose shoulders the Father laid all government; He who is the Mighty God; He who, "even when He subsisted in the form of God," "made Himself of no reputation" and became not only the Branch, but "My Servant," and in doing this has marked the pathway for every child of God. Are you God's *servant*, serving Him as your only Master, doing joyfully and eagerly His will? If in aught you have sought to follow any other master, will you submit your life, your *all* to Him, and be His Servant now?

---

117. KING OVER ALL THE EARTH

And his feet shall stand in that day upon the mount of Olives. . . . And the Lord my God shall come, and all the saints with thee. . . . And the Lord shall be king over all the earth: in that day shall there be one Lord, and his name one.
ZECHARIAH 14:4–5, 9

Some day, God grant it may be soon, "His feet shall stand upon the Mount of Olives," and ALL THE EARTH shall know that He is KING. Can any flight of swift imagination exceed that picture? Through all the strife of nations, all the pride and rivalry of kings, what peace, what glory, what undreamed of wonders shall be seen when He, "The KING of kings," shall reign "OVER ALL THE EARTH." Does that day not allure you? Does not the Spirit-given cry fill all your soul—"Even so, come, Lord Jesus!"

118. THE BRANCH

*And speak unto him, saying, Thus speaketh the L*ORD
of hosts, saying, Behold the man whose name is The
B*RANCH; and he shall grow up out of his place,*
*and he shall build the temple of the L*ORD.
ZECHARIAH 6:12

While He was here on earth *The Branch* said, "The Son
can do nothing of Himself, but what He seeth the Father
do," taking the place of humility in His utter dependence
upon God the Father. Are we tempted to exalt ourselves,
to work in some strength which He has given in the
past? Let us bow at His feet and remember that except
"ye abide in Me ye can do nothing." Let us consider
Him who, although He was the Mighty God, yet called
Himself in His earthly relationship "THE BRANCH."

---

119. JEHOVAH MY GOD

And ye shall flee by the valley of my
mountains. . .and Jehovah my God shall
come, and all the holy ones with thee.
ZECHARIAH 14:5 ASV

The Self-Existing One, seeking ever to reveal Himself to
His children and to the world that knows Him not, is
pleased and glorified when that revelation leads our souls
to cry "Jehovah, my God." If "that thing or person who
most absorbs our thought is our God," then who is my
God today? The matchless Jehovah? Or some other being
or created thing, unworthy of my trust and worship? Let

us not rest until from our inmost soul we cry, *"Jehovah, my God."*

120. THE KING

And it shall come to pass, that every one that is left
of all the nations which came against Jerusalem
shall even go up from year to year to worship the King,
the LORD of hosts, and to keep the feast of tabernacles.
ZECHARIAH 14:16

He is King, it matters not that earth refused to crown Him and to acknowledge His right to reign. He only waits the Father's day and hour to receive the kingdom which is His. The world waits and weeps, the whole creation groans in pain for lack of the conditions that shall be when men have crowned Him KING. We join that grief, but have we truly crowned Him in our lives? Does He reign supremely every day, in every act, and rule our words and thoughts? There will be joy in HIs heart, joy in Heaven, and joy in your heart, when you shall fully and with no reserve crown Jesus King and Lord of All.

121. THE MESSENGER OF THE COVENANT

Behold, I will send my messenger. . .even the messenger
of the covenant, whom ye delight in: behold,
he shall come, saith the LORD of hosts.
MALACHI 3:1

He who is our example that we should walk in His steps has called Himself "THE MESSENGER OF THE COVENANT." The Father gave a promise to those who should believe in His Son. The Son came bringing that promise, that covenant—a Messenger sent from Heaven. To the true believer that most precious covenant is, "I will write my laws upon their hearts, and upon their minds will I engrave them." Will you accept it now? "Open thy mouth wide and I will fill it."

---

122. REFINER

And he shall sit as a refiner and purifier of silver: and he shall purify the sons of Levi, and purge them as gold and silver, that they may offer unto the LORD an offering in righteousness.
MALACHI 3:3

When grosser things which men can see are removed from our lives, there is grave danger that we shall be satisfied and forget that still as the Heaven is high above the earth, so high are His ways above our ways, and His thoughts above our thoughts. That there is a finer life, a deeper, holier peace, a clearer, surer likeness of the Lord possible for His children, needs to be apprehended. And though through all of life we may seem to have been in the melting pot, shall we not say to Him again at any cost, "Dear REFINER, make me what Thou wilt. Refine me by any process that seemeth good unto Thee."

123. PURIFIER

And he shall sit as a. . .purifier of silver.
MALACHI 3:3

No work of God shows more plainly His boundless love than His desire to purify our lives. So much of dross is found in us that we have need to be tried in the furnace of affliction and to be purged as gold and silver. The difficult experiences through which we pass may often be understood as the infinite love of the Father, seeking to separate the dross from our lives, to bring us to a point of purity where we may see and reflect His image.

---

124. THE SUN OF RIGHTEOUSNESS

But unto you that fear my name shall the Sun of righteousness arise with healing in his wings.
MALACHI 4:2

Jesus said, "When the Spirit of truth is come He shall convince the world of—righteousness—because I go to the Father." Among all the sons of men "there is none righteous, no not one." But He who wrought in the creation of the worlds, and walked the streets of Judea, sits at the "right hand of the Father" in the glory. He is the Sun whose radiant righteousness heals our sin-sick souls.

Lord Jesus, we come with our earth stains and our innumerable faults and infirmities and bow at Thy feet and worship Thee while we seek the "healing in Thy wings."

125. JESUS CHRIST

The book of the generation of Jesus Christ.
MATTHEW 1:1

Here is the first title given to our Lord in the New Testament—Jesus Christ. This chapter contains a host of names, covering three periods of fourteen generations each, but *one Name* stands out like a radiant star to lighten all the others; *one Person* to whom all must render allegiance—Jesus (Saviour) Christ (the Anointed One). At His feet every knee shall bow in Heaven and on earth.

Let us pour out our hearts to Him in praise
and in prayer this day, and every day. Amen.

---

126. THE SON OF DAVID

The book of the generation of
Jesus Christ, the son of David.
MATTHEW 1:1

Our Lord was a lineal descendant of David, the king. This entitled Him to the right of sovereignty over David's land, and when He was here among men, we are told, there was no other claimant to the throne of David. Herod sought to destroy the Child-King Jesus, but Egypt was chosen as a refuge place for Him. The heart of Herod was like the hearts of all the children of men who will not have Him to rule over them. He was bearing us upon His heart, as a Child, for He is the same "yesterday, today and forever," and He is our refuge now.

Jesus Christ, Son of David, may our hearts be
linked up with Thy great heart always. Amen.

---

127. SON OF ABRAHAM

The book of the generation of Jesus
Christ. . .the son of Abraham.
MATTHEW 1:1

Three titles in one verse, "Jesus Christ—Son of David—
Son of Abraham." Abraham was the head of the covenant nation. God had given to him the promise that in
his seed should all the nations of the earth be blessed.
Jesus submitted to the Jewish law in righteousness. He
lived as a Jew, He preached to the Jews. He died for
the Jews as well as for all people. "So then they which
be of faith are blessed with faithful Abraham" (Galatians
3:9). How wonderful! God manifested in the flesh as
Abraham's seed and yet the One who made the promise
to Abraham!

Oh, Thou promised Son of Abraham and Son of God,
our Saviour, hold us fast in faith in Thy Word. Amen.

---

128. JESUS

Thou shalt call his name JESUS: for he
shall save his people from their sins.
MATTHEW 1:21

Over seven hundred times in the New Testament is this
name used—"Jesus" (Joshua). How familiar we are with

that name! Joshua of the Old Testament, who saved Israel by leading them through the River Jordan, fought their battles, and was steadfast in his allegiance to God and His people. He was a type of our Lord who is our Joshua; who fights our battles for us; who is our Leader, our Protector, our Saviour! Who will never cease His lordship until He has us safely in the sheepfold on the other side. Hallelujah, what a Saviour!

This day, Thou Saviour of our souls, in whom we are separated for eternity, guide us by Thy Holy Spirit to the praise of Thy grace. Amen.

---

129. EMMANUEL

Behold, a virgin. . .shall bring forth a son, and they shall call his name Emmanuel.
MATTHEW 1:23

This was the prophecy of Isaiah 7:14: "Therefore, the Lord Himself shall give you a sign; Behold, a virgin shall conceive, and bear a son, and shall call his name Immanuel." "Emmanuel" (God with us)! What a wonderful God and Saviour He is and He is with us as He promised in Matthew 28:19–20: "Go ye therefore, and teach all nations, baptizing them in the name of the Father, and of the Son, and of the Holy Ghost. Teaching them to observe all things whatsoever I have commanded you: and, lo, I am with you alway, even unto the end of the age." Let us sense His presence and make Him real. Walk, talk, live with and love Him more and more as the days go by.

Lord Jesus, we know that Thou dwellest in us.
May we enjoy Thy fellowship today. Amen.

---

130. A GOVERNOR

And thou Bethlehem. . .out of thee shall come
a Governor, that shall rule my people Israel.
MATTHEW 2:6

Bethlehem of Judah! A little village, twice highly honored! The birthplace of David, king of Israel, and the birthplace of Jesus the Christ, King of kings and Lord of lords! Who could visit this Land of Promise and not desire to see this city of cities, the place where Jehovah enthroned in human form and lying in a manger gazed into the face of the virgin Mary, His mother. The government shall be upon His shoulders and He will reign in righteousness. Blessed day!

We pray for its soon coming, and ask
for grace that we may hasten it. Amen.

---

131. THE YOUNG CHILD

When they had heard the king, they departed; and, lo, the
star, which they saw in the east, went before them, till it
came and stood over where the young child was.
MATTHEW 2:9

A star in the East led the Wise Men to a Star that shall outshine all the stars of Heaven. Look at this Young Child!

Hold fast your attention as you gaze upon His face, lying there, His eyes looking into your own inquiring eyes. Visualize, if you can, God manifested in the flesh for you. God—the Young Child! The Creator of all things! Before whom are thirty years of human life in which He will toil with His fellow men. Mystery of mysteries!

Oh, Thou wonderful One, as we bow before Thee today, help us to discern something of Thy devotion for the sons of men. Amen.

---

132. A NAZARENE

And he came and dwelt in a city called Nazareth: that it might be fulfilled which was spoken by the prophets, He shall be called a Nazarene.

MATTHEW 2:23

Nazareth was a town in the northern border of the plain of Esdraelon. Here came the angel Gabriel and announced to Mary the coming birth of Christ: "And the angel came in unto her, and said, Hail, thou that art highly favoured, the Lord is with thee: blessed art thou among women" (Luke 1:26–28). On the night of His betrayal Our Lord asked the question, "Whom seek ye?" They replied, "Jesus of Nazareth," and He said, "I am He."

Jesus of Nazareth, may we never be ashamed to be called the followers of the lowly Nazarene.

133. FRIEND OF SINNERS

Behold. . .a friend of publicans and sinners.
MATTHEW 11:19

These are the words of Jesus Himself. He quotes their own phrases as applied to Himself. What a title! How wonderfully true it is—"A Friend of Sinners"! So He was and so He is—a Friend that sticketh closer than a brother. Laying aside the royal robes of Heaven, He came here to befriend sinful men. It was a life-work that cost Him His life. Hallelujah! What a Friend! How gladly He paid the price of friendship. As we take up the work of the day, let us ask ourselves the question, "Am I a friend of sinners?" If not, then I am not like my Lord, for He was and He joyed in it.

Lord Jesus, the world is full of friendless sinners.
May we make them acquainted with Thee
who art their Friend. Amen.

---

134. THE SERVANT OF JEHOVAH

Behold my servant, whom I have chosen.
MATTHEW 12:18

Jesus, the prophesied Servant! Isaiah had portrayed Him. Jehovah had chosen Him. All of God's ways were known unto Him from the beginning. You hear the echo of His voice, "I delight to do Thy will, O my God!" Nothing was too great for Him to do, for He was the Creator, and nothing was too hard for Him, for He had all power.

Nothing was too small for Him to do, for He stooped to notice a widow's mite and give a mighty lesson from it. What a gracious privilege to be yoked with Him in service.

Dear Lord, let us labor with Thee,
the "Servant of Jehovah," today and thus
make it a good day for Thee. Amen.

---

135. MY BELOVED

Behold. . .my beloved, in whom
my soul is well pleased.
MATTHEW 12:18

Twenty-seven times in the Song of Solomon is this title used of our Lord. God's Son was a *beloved* Servant. How dear He was to the Father—dear as the apple of His eye. Yet His love for us was manifest in the surrender of His Son to pay the penalty of our sin. "Greater love hath no man than this." "While we were yet sinners, Christ died for us." In the hour of darkness He cried, "My God, My God, why hast Thou forsaken Me?" The agony, the grief, the pain He suffered, all had a voice which rings out the message, "God so loved."

Our Father, Thy love for us has broken all the barriers
down; and we pray that Thy Spirit may rest upon us this
day as we meditate upon the greatness of Thy love. Amen.

136. A SOWER

He that soweth the good seed is the Son of man.
MATTHEW 13:37

The seed is the Word of God. God's Son sowed the good seed. He soweth the Word of Truth in the hearts of men. When we sow the Gospel we sow good seed. When we give out the Word of God we are sowing good seed. Nothing is comparable to the *Word* itself. It has potential power. It is a *living* seed and never fails. We are to imitate our Lord, the Sower, and see that the pure seed of the Word is scattered wherever we go. "Sow beside all waters."

Lord, make me a seed-sower this day, and hear my prayer for all the sowers in all the world. Amen!

---

137. THE CHRIST

Thou art the Christ, the Son of the living God.
MATTHEW 16:16

This is the title of the long-looked-for Saviour—the Anointed One. Prophets had foretold His coming and now His kingly authority is recorded. Over three hundred times is this title used in the New Testament. From "Christ" comes the word, "Christian," and from "Christian" comes the word, "Christianity." Today this land of ours is the foremost Christian nation of the world. Our Gospel is the Gospel of Christ of which we are not ashamed, for it is the power of God unto salvation to everyone that believeth.

*Lord, as "Christ-ones" let us honor Thee by having
the same anointing power resting upon us as
we enter the service of the day. Amen.*

---

138. JESUS THE CHRIST

*Then charged he his disciples that they should
tell no man that he was Jesus the Christ.*
MATTHEW 16:20

This title, "Jesus the Christ," is used a hundred times
in the New Testament. "The Saviour—the Anointed
One"—a combination that magnifies the office of the
One whom we long to worship. The time had not yet
come for them to preach the story of redemption. They
were to hold their peace for a season, but He tells *us* to
go into all the world and tell to all people the wonderful
message of Jesus Christ and His finished work. Are we
obeying the command?

*Dear Father, as we go forth today with this precious Name
in our hearts and on our lips, help us to tell someone of the
wonders of the Man, Thy Son, Jesus the Christ! Amen.*

---

139. MY BELOVED SON

*This is my beloved Son, in whom
I am well pleased; hear ye him.*
MATTHEW 17:5

Wonderful manifestation! A cloud of glory overshadow-
ing that which was too deep for human eyes to penetrate.

The voice of Jehovah attesting that Jesus was His beloved Son and that His words were to be heard. The same voice and the same message were heard in Chapter 3:17 when our Lord was baptized, and once again in John 12:28 in the Garden. "*His* beloved" and *our* beloved! How marvellous is that testimony to Him whom we have learned to love, and because we love Him, we are beloved of the Father.

Lord, may we breathe it over and over again today,
"I am my beloved's and my beloved is mine." Amen.

---

140. THE PROPHET OF NAZARETH

This is Jesus the prophet of Nazareth of Galilee.
Matthew 21:11

This great demonstration had been planned by God and foretold by Him (Zechariah 9:9). Our Lord comes into Jerusalem riding upon the foal of an ass. The crowd is vast; the enthusiasm is great. "Who is this?" is the cry; and the answer is, "This is Jesus, the Prophet of Nazareth." A despised Nazarene! A prophet from an obscure village! We are all proud if, perchance, we were born in some noted place; but God, when He took the form of a man, was born in a manger and made His home in Nazareth. For our sakes He became poor, that we through His poverty, might be made rich.

Let us meditate upon the riches of His grace, bow at His feet and kiss them as we adore Him; and may we walk humbly this day with the despised Nazarene. Amen.

141. MASTER

One is your Master, even Christ;
and all ye are brethren.
MATTHEW 23:8

"Master" here means "Teacher," or some say, "Leader." The admonition is to avoid the desire for personal distinction so common among God's leaders. Let our eyes be fixed upon Him and depend upon the Holy Spirit who represents Him, and who guides us into *all* truth (John 16:13–14). The more we seek to exalt Him, the less will we think of magnifying ourselves. Make Him Master of your life today, remembering that "The disciple is not above his master; but everyone that is perfect shall be as his master" (Luke 6:40).

O, that we may be as our Master, the meek and
lowly One! For this day, our Lord, we need great
grace as we seek to follow Thee as Master. Amen.

---

142. THE BRIDEGROOM

And while they went to buy, the bridegroom came.
MATTHEW 25:10

The Bridegroom must come. The true church is His beloved espoused bride. He has waited a long, long time for her to prepare herself for the glad day and to add the last one which will complete the body. Are you thinking of Him today as the Coming One? And of yourself as one of those who are to be blessed as His beloved throughout eternity? How insignificant are all the little cares and trials! How small they seem when our eyes are turned with expectancy toward Him as He comes in the clouds. "Blessed are they which are called unto the marriage supper of the Lamb" (Revelation 19:9). Hallelujah!

May our prayer always be, "Even so, come, Lord Jesus, come quickly." Amen.

---

143. THE HOLY ONE OF GOD

I know thee who thou art, the Holy One of God.
MARK 1:24

What a testimony coming from the lips of one possessed of an unclean spirit, Satan's tool, under his power. But the presence of Christ overawed him. "I know Thee who Thou art, the Holy One of God." This was not a willing testimony, but was forced from him. Many men are devil-possessed, and the devil has powers accorded him, but Christ can hinder his followers; can cast out his demons and forbid their speaking (verse 34). How lovingly we should bow at His feet—the Holy One of God! May we fix our thoughts upon Him and say many times today as we walk and talk with Him,

"Oh, Thou Holy One of God, glorify Thyself through us." Amen.

144. OUR BROTHER

For whosoever shall do the will of God,
the same is my brother.

MARK 3:35

If this is true, and it is, then the reverse is also true, and He is our Brother. The picture is given in the thirty-first and thirty-fourth verses: "There came then His brethren and His mother, and, standing without, sent unto Him, calling him. . . . And He looked round about on them which sat about Him, and said, Behold My mother and My brethren." How wonderful that He should graciously give this title to those who do the Father's will! And what is that will? The acceptance of His Son as our Saviour and Lord, and the submission of our will to His will as revealed in His Word, for His Word is His will. How near and dear He is to us, our Lord and our Brother! Hold it fast in your meditation—"Ours by faith; ours forever."

Dear Lord, keep us in loving fellowship
with Thyself this day. Amen.

---

145. THOU SON OF THE MOST HIGH GOD

And cried with a loud voice, and said, What have I to
do with thee, Jesus, thou Son of the most high God?

MARK 5:7

Here we are confronted with another testimony from an unclean spirit—"Son of the most high God," he calls

Jesus. What unseen powers compelled this significant title? Was it brought about by being face to face with Himself? Judas betrayed Him, but this poor, demon-possessed man worshipped Him. In these strange days many teachers, professors and preachers refuse to honor Him as *the Son*, but only as *a Son* of God. But we lift our hearts to Him and say,

"Son of the most high God, be our companion this day and may we withhold naught from Thee." Amen.

146. THE CARPENTER

Is not this the carpenter. . . ?
MARK 6:3

The Carpenter! Two things are suggested in this verse. Joseph is not mentioned and is probably not now living. Jesus is working at the carpenter's bench and continued to do so until He assumed His place in His public ministry. We can and should visualize Him in His daily tasks—a man among men. How near He seems to us! What a joy to know that He handled the hammer and sharpened the saw, planed the plank and helped to supply the food for the family. Test this picture of Him with any false system and observe the contrast. No matter what our calling may be, the Carpenter will be one with us. We can walk arm in arm with Him to the daily task.

*O, Thou Carpenter of Galilee,
be Thou our ideal always! Amen.*

147. THE SON OF MARY

Is not this. . .the son of Mary. . . ?
MARK 6:3

The Carpenter, the "Son of Mary," has come back to His hometown from an evangelistic trip in which He had worked many miracles. The people were astonished at His teaching. Prejudice possessed them. "Is not this the Son of Mary?" We never worship Mary as do our Catholic friends, but we do honor her above all women—God's chosen vessel to bring forth His Son and fulfill His prophecy. How true He was to the last. See Him on the cross and hear His last words to Mary, "Woman, behold thy son" (John, the beloved, to whom He had said, "Behold thy mother").

Blessed title—Son of Mary! The Babe who is one day to rule the world and at whose feet we shall bow in worshipful adoration! Let us do so now. Amen.

148. GOOD MASTER

Good Master, what shall I do that I may inherit eternal life?
MARK 10:17

This question was asked of our Lord by a young man with great possessions, as recorded in Matthew 19:17. This is the concrete question of the soul of man, "What shall I *do* to secure a right to Heaven?" The theme of *religion* is *do*; but the theme of our Lord was just the opposite,

"Follow Me." Eternal life is a gift. Those who accept and follow Him find that He *is* the "Good Master" because He is the "God-Master," for only One is good and He is God, and He has provided for us a salvation—simple to accept but costing Him a price which involved His own life. How gracious is our God and how we should love and adore Him!

Lord, may we walk in the
sunshine of Thy love today. Amen.

---

149. SON OF MAN

The Son of man shall be delivered unto the chief priests,
and unto the scribes; and they shall condemn him to death.
MARK 10:33

In the ninth chapter Jesus had said, "The Son of Man is delivered into the hands of men and they shall kill Him." How earnestly He sought to stress the fact of His approaching sacrifice upon His disciples and how He longed for their sympathy; but, alas, alas, how hard is the human heart! How difficult it is for Him to win us to Himself! "The Son of Man must suffer many things," He had said, but the saddest of all was the failure of His own beloved disciples to enter into the burden He bore as He approached the cross.

Oh, Thou Holy Son of Man, give unto
us the loving hearts that will enter into
fellowship with Thee in all things. Amen.

150. A RANSOM

The Son of man came. . .to give
his life a ransom for many.
MARK 10:45

"A Ransom for many"! Here Christ is set forth as the penalty paid for the sins of the world. As sinners under the judgment wrath of God, He took our place and paid the penalty and the price of our deliverance with His own blood. Listen to the drops of blood as they fall from hands and feet and wounded side! They voice the words, "The ransom price for *my* sins and for the sins of the whole world." Would that men everywhere would believe it and receive it. How dear, how precious is He to us, washed clean in His blood and freed forever from the punishment due us.

Lord, may our ransomed souls well up
in praise to Thy glorious Name! Amen.

151. ONE SON, HIS WELL BELOVED

Having yet therefore one son, his wellbeloved, he sent him
also last unto them, saying, They will reverence my son.
MARK 12:6

The Saviour is in Jerusalem. The chief priests and scribes come to Him and question His authority. Jesus answers them in the parable of the vineyard, picturing to them the treatment of the servants who were sent to gather the fruit, telling the story—so old, so strange—of the attitude of the human heart toward God. He sent His Son, His well-beloved Son, and they took Him and killed Him and cast Him out. How could they? They have cast Him out of the schools and many of the churches, though all we have of earthly civilization and comforts today we owe to Him.

God's Well-beloved Son, we enthrone Thee today in our hearts. Help us to worship and adore Thee. Amen.

---

152. CHRIST, THE SON OF THE BLESSED

Art thou the Christ, the Son of the Blessed?
MARK 14:61

The court is convened. The High Priest is presiding. Charges had been brought against the Lord Jesus Christ by false witnesses but they had not agreed. The High Priest put to Him a question, "Art Thou the Christ, the Son of the Blessed?" And He answered, "I am." There was no denial of the title, but a straight confession of His Sonship, Heirship, Power and coming Glory. And when He comes—if He tarry yet a season—we will be among those who will be caught up in the clouds to meet Him in the air and with the hosts of Heaven acclaim Him "Blessed"!

*Lord, Jesus Christ, Thou Son of the Blessed,
hasten the glad day. Amen.*

153. THE KING OF THE JEWS

And Pilate asked him, Art thou the King of the Jews?
And he answering said unto them, Thou sayest it.
MARK 15:2

What a title for our Lord to put His seal upon at the time when the Jews were in subjection to the Romans and He Himself a prisoner before a judge. But He *is* King of the Jews—yes, *King of kings and Lord of all*. Pilate will yet stand before Him to be judged, and the Jewish people will yet proclaim Him as their own King. He is the Ruler. Let us give Him His rightful place as Ruler in our lives. How can we serve Him today? Perhaps in some definite prayer for the Jewish people and some testimony to them of the joy there is in knowing, loving, and serving Him.

Lord, remember Thine ancient people and all
who seek to make Thee known to them. Amen.

---

154. THE SON OF THE HIGHEST

He shall be great, and shall be
called the Son of the Highest.
LUKE 1:32

This is the message of the angel to Mary and here is a remarkable coincidence. In Mark 5:7, we have the evil spirit in the man in the tombs giving a similar title to Jesus, "Son of the Most High God." The title here given Him is in fulfillment of Psalm 132:11: "The LORD hath sworn in truth unto David; he will not turn from it; of the fruit of thy body will I set upon thy throne." David's heir is to reign as Son of the Most High God, and that time only waits for the completion of the church which is His Body. Let us do our best each day to win souls for Him and thus hasten the day when we shall be with Him and reign with Him.

Son of the Highest, we bow to Thee, we worship Thee.
Help us to magnify Thy name today. Amen.

155. GOD MY SAVIOUR

And my spirit hath rejoiced
in God my Saviour.
LUKE 1:47

The word "Saviour" here is "Soter," meaning "presence." Should we not imitate Mary, the blessed woman, in magnifying our Saviour and rejoicing in the finished work which He hath wrought in our behalf? It is never what *we* are but what *He* is. Our joy is in Him and we rejoice with joy unspeakable and full of glory as we face this day with joyful hearts. Shall we not have a tender heart for those who do not know Him?

Saviour, like a shepherd lead us today to glorify
Thy name in our efforts to win souls for Thee. Amen.

156. HORN OF SALVATION

And hath raised up an horn of salvation
for us in the house of his servant David.
LUKE 1:69

Here is a title which suggests the strength and power of our Lord—"Horn of Salvation." The word "horn" as used in the Scripture signifies "strength" and is often found in Hebrew literature. In the horns, the bull manifests his strength. The Lord Jesus Christ is our Strength and a very present help in time of trouble (Psalms 118:14; 92:10; 28:7; 37:39). "But the salvation of the righteous is of the Lord; He is their strength in the time of trouble." You may be tempted and tried today. You may have burdens to bear. Let Him be your "Horn of salvation."

Lord, strengthen us by the power of Thy
might for today's service for Thee. Amen.

---

157. THE HIGHEST

And thou, child, shalt be called
the prophet of the Highest.
LUKE 1:76

Listen to the voice of Zacharias, father of John the Baptist, as he voices the wonderful prophecy concerning his son who was to be the prophet of the Lord to prepare the way before Him. Our Lord is here named "the Highest," or, better, "the Most High." He came from the heights of glory to be born in a manger. "Prophet" in the New Testament means "a public expounder" and to us, His redeemed ones, has been committed this honorable title. We are the expounders of this great revelation of the Bible concerning our most highly exalted LORD.

Glory to God in the Highest, King of kings and
Lord of lords, whom we claim as our own. Amen.

158. THE DAYSPRING FROM ON HIGH

Through the tender mercy of our God; whereby
the dayspring from on high hath visited us.
LUKE 1:78

Zacharias is inspired as his soul goes forth to speak of the coming of the Messiah. It has been suggested that the glory of the sunrise was breaking over the hills surrounding Jerusalem and the golden glory lighted up the horizon as his lips breathed the words inspired by the Spirit of God, "Dayspring from on high"! Perhaps the morning glory brought to the mind of Zacharias the message of Isaiah, "Arise, shine, for thy light is come and the glory of the Lord is risen upon thee."

Before we take up our daily tasks, let us turn our
eyes to the heavens with grateful hearts and let
the Holy Spirit flood our souls with the glory
of the Risen, Coming Christ. Amen.

159. CHRIST, THE LORD

*For unto you is born this day in the city of
David a Saviour, which is Christ the Lord.*
LUKE 2:11

The heavens are opened now and the message of the
angel of the Lord is announced—"good tidings of great
joy." The message was to the humble shepherds and it
will mean much to us if we can, in humility of heart,
take our place with the shepherds, acknowledge our
unworthiness, and appropriate the truth to our own
souls—"Unto you is born a Saviour, Christ the Lord"
(the Anointed One—the Ruler). We are no longer to
rule ourselves. He is to rule us.

*Lord, with joy we submit our wills, and surrender
all to Thee. Help us to magnify Thee this day. Amen.*

---

160. THE BABE

*Ye shall find the babe wrapped in
swaddling clothes, lying in a manger.*
LUKE 2:12

Again the voice of the angel rings out to the shepherds:
"Christ the Lord—The Babe—lying in a manger." How
easy it would be for the shepherds to find Him. No other
newly born babe would be found "lying in a manger"—
just One—and He, the altogether lovely One, the chiefest
among ten thousand! Sometimes the saints magnify their
human birthright and place of birth, but He was to be

a blessing to the humblest. Would not the cattle—could they have sensed the significance of the event—have bent their knees in homage to the Babe? How sad to know that millions in our land have not yet bowed the knee to Him.

Lord, may we who have named Thy name, bow in humblest submission to Thee today and pour out our hearts in joyful praise to Thee, Thou Babe of Bethlehem. Amen.

161. THE CONSOLATION OF ISRAEL

There was a man in Jerusalem, whose name was Simeon; and the same man was just and devout, waiting for the consolation of Israel.

LUKE 2:25

Simeon was just and devout and waited for the "Consolation of Israel." "Consolation" means "paraclete" (One coming alongside) as we think and speak of the Holy Spirit who comes to abide in and lead us out in our daily life. Simeon was waiting for the deliverance of the Jews by the coming of the Messiah. They did not as a nation receive Him, but some did and were consoled, and Israel shall yet have the promised consolation, as Paul was comforted by the power of the indwelling Holy Spirit (1 Thessalonians 1:5).

Lord, may we also rely upon the abiding comfort of the indwelling of the Holy Spirit all the day. Amen.

162. THE LORD'S CHRIST

And it was revealed unto him by the Holy Ghost, that he should not see death, before he had seen the Lord's Christ.
LUKE 2:26

Simeon was a just and devout man who believed the Word of God and rested upon its promises. The Holy Ghost came upon him and made a revelation to him. He was not to taste of death until he had tasted the sweets of seeing and knowing "the Lord's Christ." The Lord never fails His loved ones. When He can get hold of the hearts of men and women He is glad to make a revelation of Himself to them and give unto them the power of the Holy Spirit. His great heart beats in sympathy with every pulsing of every loyal-hearted follower.

Holy Spirit, give us new spiritual visions of the Lord's Christ. Amen.

---

163. THE SALVATION OF GOD

For mine eyes have seen thy salvation.
LUKE 2:30

The aged saint Simeon, standing in the temple, took the child Jesus in his arms and, looking into His face, lifted his eyes to Heaven and said: "Lord, now lettest thou thy servant depart in peace, according to thy word; for *mine eyes have seen thy salvation.*" Long had he waited, long had he prayed, long had he desired to see Him. Now the Spirit of God reveals unto him the fact that his heart's desire had been granted and that he was gazing upon the Divine Saviour of souls and death had no more terrors for him. There is but one cure for the world's unrest, "The Salvation of God." Let us go out today and tell the story wherever we can. The poor, hungry-hearted, sin-sick souls are waiting.

Lord, guide us in this service to Thy Glory. Amen.

---

164. A LIGHT TO LIGHTEN THE GENTILES

A light to lighten the Gentiles,
and the glory of thy people Israel.
LUKE 2:32

The world has been a dark world ever since Adam and Eve listened to the temptation of Satan. There was no hope until God said: "The seed of the woman shall bruise the serpent's head"—a promise of coming victory for a lost race. He who is the light of the Gentiles is the light of the world (Matthew 4:16). The light shone for Israel first, but Israel rejected its blessed beams. But again the Light shall shine for the people now wandering over the earth in darkness. What is the duty of believers? Is it not to lift the Light high so that the world of sinners in darkness may come into fellowship with Him?

Lord of Light, help us to shine as
lights in a dark world, this day. Amen.

165. THE GLORY OF
THY PEOPLE ISRAEL

A light to lighten the Gentiles,
and the glory of thy people Israel.
LUKE 2:32

The message of Paul was "To the Jew first," but here the Gentiles are mentioned first. The Jews turned away from Jesus and would not have Him to rule over them, but the Gentiles will not receive Him, either—just a few. The glory shall rest upon Israel when He comes with sceptre in hand to rule a reconstructed earth. The Shekinah glory, manifested in the tabernacle and temple, will shine again upon His beloved people and Jesus—the Jew—will be the glory of Israel in that day. Let us love the Jews and seek to bring the Gospel of the grace of God to them.

Lord Jesus, who art the Glory of Thy People Israel,
remember Thy persecuted, penalty-paying people
and help us to love them. Amen.

---

166. A SIGN

This child is set. . .for a sign
which shall be spoken against.
LUKE 2:34

Our Lord Jesus Christ was a significant sign to Israel. The prophecies had long before made clear that Israel was to be tested when the Messiah came. Some would believe and follow Him. Some would reject and crucify Him. Our Lord gave testimony to this fact when Pilate asked Him, "Art Thou a King?" And His answer was: "To this end was I born and for this cause came I into the world." Poor Pilate, he had his evidence but would not accept it. Where is he? The Sign has been given to our land, also. Where are the multitudes? The same old story will be told again and again.

Oh, Lord, have compassion upon this poor land. Inspire thy servants to be brave and true in sounding the alarm. Amen.

---

167. THE CHILD JESUS

The child Jesus tarried behind in Jerusalem.

LUKE 2:43

Here we have our first view of Jesus as a young lad, interested in the business of His Heavenly Father. Hear Him when Joseph and Mary seek Him: "Wist ye not that I must be about my Father's business?" The strangeness of the story of His life is a constant surprise. God manifested in the flesh—a Child—with words of wisdom falling from His lips—a message for us all, "Occupy (do business) till I come." Every disciple is a business man or woman, and our business is the most important in all the world. Let us take as a motto for our daily life the words of the Child Jesus, "I must be about my Father's business."

Lord, help us to be busy about Thy business this day. Amen.

168. PHYSICIAN

And he said unto them, Ye will surely say
unto me this proverb, Physician, heal thyself.
LUKE 4:23

Our Lord had been in Galilee. His fame had spread throughout that region. He had wrought mighty miracles. He comes back home to Nazareth where He had been brought up, and preached in the synagogue on the Sabbath Day from Isaiah 61:1–3, saying, "This day is this Scripture fulfilled in your ears." The people who heard these words, said, "Is not this Joseph's son?" and then Jesus quoted to them our verse, a proverb among the Jews. What a mistake they made. He *was* the Great Physician. He *is* the Great Physician—"Able to do exceeding abundantly above all we can ask or think." How few know Him as such a One! How few look to Him! How few depend upon Him!

Lord, Thou who art the Great Physician, we look
to Thee today to supply our every need. Amen.

---

169. LORD OF THE SABBATH

And he said unto them, That the Son
of man is Lord also of the sabbath.
LUKE 6:5

He is the Master (Lord) of the Sabbath. He is the Maker of Heaven and earth. "Without Him nothing was made that is made." He is either what He claimed to be, or else He is the greatest impostor that ever lived. The Sabbath was made for man, and not man for the Sabbath. It is lawful to do good on the Sabbath. Serving others is serving the Lord of the Sabbath. He, with His disciples, plucked and ate the wheat on the Sabbath, and on the Sabbath He healed the man with the withered hand. The Sabbath is the Lord's Day. Solve all your problems in connection with the Sabbath Day by the question, "What would the Lord do on this day?" Then whatsoever you do, whether ye eat or drink, do all to the glory of God.

Lord Jesus, we pray that every day may be a good day for Thee through our lives. Amen.

---

170. A GREAT PROPHET

And they glorified God, saying, That a great prophet is risen up among us; and, That God hath visited his people.
LUKE 7:16

Four centuries had elapsed since Malachi had passed away, and Israel had been without a prophetic voice. Now they are stirred by the presence of Jesus and glorify God. Israel was not forsaken. God's Word was true. And Jesus was a great Prophet; yes, greater even than they knew. Humble, quiet, gentle, no pomp, no display, but wonderful in works. Do *we* recognize His greatness? Do we believe His prophecies and promises? Do we possess them and profit by them and give glory to His name?

Lord, help us to believe every word of the Prophetic Book. Amen.

171. THE CHRIST OF GOD

He said unto them, But whom say ye that I am?
Peter answering said, The Christ of God.
LUKE 9:20

Jesus was alone in prayer and asked His disciples the question, "Whom say the people that I am?" and after they had given their answers, He asked the question in our text. The disciples were compelled to recognize His heavenly gifts, His greatness, His power and His gracious Spirit, but it was hard for them to think of Him as One who must suffer persecution and death at the hands of the Jews. But He knew all that was before Him and walked steadily on toward the cruel cross upon which He must die. Today the *professing* church is inclined to reject the theme of His atoning blood, but those of us to whom He is "the Christ of God" adore Him more and more as the depths of His sacrifice and suffering are revealed.

Lord, may we hold Thee in our hearts
today as "the Christ of God." Amen.

---

172. A CERTAIN SAMARITAN

But a certain Samaritan, as he
journeyed. . .had compassion on him.
LUKE 10:33

The story of the Good Samaritan is familiar to all of us, but read it again. Here we take the liberty of viewing our Lord as "a certain Samaritan." Humanity was His neighbor. He loved all, lived for all, labored for all, and laid down His life for all. Being what He was and is, He could be nothing less, and we look up to Him today and glory in the mightiness of His humanity and the magnificence of His heart. If we are indeed Spirit-born, then there must be something of His loving kindness in us, and the world is waiting for our touch upon it. Will we take the Good Samaritan for our model today and pray,

"Lord Jesus, make us more like Thyself." Amen.

---

173. THE MASTER OF THE HOUSE

When once the master of the house is risen up. . .he shall answer and say unto you, I know you not whence ye are.
LUKE 13:25

Here is a new title for our Lord—"Master of the House." How appropriate it is—"Lord of the house—the Head—the Governor." The "house" is Heaven where He is to rule. The appeal is for earnest effort upon the part of believers to impress upon the unsaved the fact that there is a Heaven and there is a hell, and only *one gate* to Heaven—Jesus Christ. Why do we not make more definite to people the awful consequences of failure to hear His voice *now*, and that there will come a time when it will be too late?

Dear Lord, may we labor and pray earnestly today that we may be faithful in urging upon people the necessity of decision for Christ. Amen.

174. A GUEST

And when they saw it, they all murmured, saying,
That he was gone to be guest with a man that is a sinner.
LUKE 19:7

Zaccheus was highly honored when Christ invited Himself to be his Guest. How like our Lord! He knew Zaccheus wanted to see Him, and He sought him out and became his guest. How we would congratulate ourselves were some noted person to come to our house to dine. What a fuss we would make. How we would boast about it. Why do we not tell the story to everybody "A Great One has come to live in my house"? "Who is He?" "He is the King of glory. He holds the worlds in the hollow of His hand. He lives with me."

Oh, Thou blessed Guest, help us today to
magnify and glorify Thee before all. Amen.

---

175. A CERTAIN NOBLEMAN

He said therefore, A certain nobleman went into a far
country to receive for himself a kingdom, and to return.
LUKE 19:12

The setting of this picture is remarkable. Our Lord is standing with the Jews around Him, in the shadow of a palace built by a nobleman, Archelaus, who had gone to Rome and received the kingdom from Caesar. Our Lord is the Nobleman whose face was turned toward the land beyond the skies where He has gone and from whence He will one day return. "Occupy till I come" is His message. He has entrusted to us, as His servants, the most valuable treasures of Heaven—time, opportunity, the gifts of the Holy Spirit, a great wide world in which to transact the greatest of all business! Precious privileges are ours and a solemn accounting must be given.

Lord, give us keenness of vision to see,
and wisdom to utilize our opportunities in
the investment of our lives for Thee. Amen.

---

176. THE CHOSEN OF GOD

Let him save himself, if he
be Christ, the chosen of God.
LUKE 23:35

Christ is on the cross. He prays, "Father, forgive them." The people stand beholding Him, the rulers deride Him and mock Him. What a picture! What a slur! "*If* thou be the Christ, the *chosen of God*"? So do men today. The question mark grows as the days go by, but the title which was given Him in derision is a wonderfully true one, and is found again in 1 Peter 2:4. Yes, indeed! Chosen before the foundation of the earth, and the *only One* who could be chosen for the great work of our redemption.

Lord, Thou has chosen HIM, and Thou has chosen US.
May we adore and glory in Thee this day. Amen.

177. A PROPHET MIGHTY IN DEED AND WORD

And he said unto them, What things? And they said unto him, Concerning Jesus of Nazareth, which was a prophet mighty in deed and word before God and all the people.

LUKE 24:19

Some hated Him. Some worshipped Him. Mighty in life, mighty in death, and mighty in His resurrection! The rulers thought they had eliminated Him. Some seek to do so today. They crucified Him in fulfillment of Scripture, but He is alive today. He lives in the hearts of millions who would be willing to be crucified for Him. He will live throughout the eternal ages and every word He ever uttered will be fulfilled to the letter.

O Thou mighty Prophet, help us to lay hold of the Word with intensified faith and hold fast until Thou shalt come. Amen.

---

178. THE WORD

In the beginning was the Word, and the Word was with God, and the Word was God.

JOHN 1:1

We come today to John's Gospel in which we shall find many titles for the Son of God. Here we confront the first—"The Word." The book of Genesis commences with creation, but John commences with the Creator. Back of all things with which we ever have had or will have to do is *the Word*. "The Word was God!" What a foundation for our faith when we know that Jesus was the Word and the Word was God. Every day we can, if we will, be facing this tremendous fact, and as we feel the throb of our heart, there is a voice which says, "God!" As we look upon the heavens and the clouds—"God!" The sun, the moon, the trees, the flowers, the living creatures, all are saying, "God!" Without Him—nothing! With Him—all things!

Oh, Thou Living Word, who hast given us the written Word, help us to abide in Thee today. Amen.

179. THE LIGHT OF MEN

In him was life; and the life was the light of men.
JOHN 1:4

God said, "Let there be light: and there was light" (Genesis 1:3). All life proceeds from our Lord, and all light, also. The Word is a life and light-giving Word— "The light of the world is Jesus." Visualize the whole world in the darkness of sin, men groping blindly, restless and hopeless. *We* have the Light of Life. *We* see Him face-to-face. *We* bask in the sunshine of His glory. Pity the blind! Pray for the blind! Carry the light of the glorious Gospel to their darkened souls. Tell them to arise and shine for the Light is come and the glory of the Lord shall shine upon them.

Help us, Lord, to walk in the light as we have fellowship with Thee and with one another. Amen.

180. THE TRUE LIGHT

*That was the true Light, which lighteth
every man that cometh into the world.*

JOHN 1:9

"The *true* Light." This is in contrast with *false* lights. How many there are in our day. Satan is busy sending them forth through false cults, false teachers, and false teaching. False lights dazzle the eyes but never reveal truth, nor bring radiance to the soul. The gloom of sin, the uncertainty of life, the dark outlook for the future, confront the sinner, stumbling along, without God and without hope. God has ordained us as lights. Let our lights shine today, and may we help some blinded ones to see Jesus as the true Light of the World.

*Lord Jesus, in the light of Thy Word, and in the light
of Thyself, may we witness for Thee today. Amen.*

---

181. THE ONLY BEGOTTEN
OF THE FATHER

*And the Word was made flesh, and dwelt among us,
(and we beheld his glory, the glory as of the only
begotten of the Father,) full of grace and truth.*

JOHN 1:14

This is the most sublime of all the statements of Scripture—"God became flesh!" John saw His glory. How wonderful! That glory was manifest in the person of the Only Begotten of the Father—Jesus Christ. He is the Unique Figure in the world's history—the sinless, perfect One—perfect God and perfect Man. "Great is the mystery of godliness; God was manifest in the flesh." He must be God to forgive sin, and He must be Man to atone for sin. So the God-Man is our Saviour.

We worship Thee, we adore Thee, O Thou only begotten of the Father. Help us to walk and talk with Thee this day. Amen.

---

182. THE LAMB OF GOD

The next day John seeth Jesus coming unto him, and saith, Behold the Lamb of God, which taketh away the sin of the world.

JOHN 1:29

How shall we say in a few words that which springs up in our hearts and would break forth from our lips? "The Lamb which beareth away our sin" is a better rendering, for He takes it away by *bearing* it. He *bore* the sins of those who received Him while here on the earth and He bore them *away* when He paid the penalty on the cross and shed His atoning blood. *God's* Lamb! No one else could be God's Lamb. He was the *voluntary* offering. What can we do? Believe it, accept it, take our place with Him.

Let us behold Thee every day—Jesus Thou Lamb of God—counting nothing too good to give to Thee or too much to do for Thee. Amen.

183. THE SON OF GOD

And I saw, and bare record
that this is the Son of God.
JOHN 1:34

John had not known Him as the Messiah although he did know Him to be Mary's Son. But when the Holy Spirit descended upon Jesus at His baptism, John knew Him as the Son of God and bore record to the fact. The testimony of John the Baptist is clear! Jesus is God's Son. He is the Promised One. Not *a* Son of God, as some of our learned critics condescendingly say, but *the* Son of God. We should seek to be like John the Baptist—a sign-post pointing to Him and saying, "Behold! the Son of God." John laid down his life for his loyalty to the Son of God. May we be willing to suffer anything so that our testimony shall be clear and clean always for Him.

Lord, help us to point someone to Thee today. Amen.

---

184. RABBI

Nathanael answered and saith unto him, Rabbi,
thou art the Son of God; thou art the King of Israel.
JOHN 1:49

"Rabbi" means "teacher" and is used seven times in the New Testament. Nathanael recognized Christ as a teacher and He was—the greatest Teacher that ever lived. A careful study of the four Gospels with a view to learning how Christ taught, His method, His manner, and His purpose, is better than any other possible training for Bible teachers. Christ was a true teacher. He taught the truth. He condescended to men of low estate. He used words which men could understand. He illustrated His messages in a practical manner. "The common people heard him gladly." That was a high compliment indeed.

Lord, help us to teach by our lips and by our life.
Let us pray that we may so teach today. Amen.

---

185. THE KING OF ISRAEL

Nathanael answered and saith unto him,
Rabbi. . .thou art the King of Israel.
JOHN 1:49

When Philip found Nathanael, the latter said to him, "Can any good thing come out of Nazareth?" But when Nathanael came in touch with Jesus he broke out in testimony to His Deity and His Messiahship. Our Lord did not fail to acknowledge this sterling testimony and a great promise was given to Nathanael, "Hereafter thou shalt see the heavens opened and the angels of God ascending and descending." Ministering spirits were to be seen by him. Prayers were to ascend in the name of Christ and answers were to come back through Christ. We also can see the open heavens if we have faith.

Let us send up our prayers today in
His name and look for the answer. Amen.

186. HIS ONLY BEGOTTEN SON

*For God so loved the world, that he gave his only
begotten Son, that whosoever believeth in him
should not perish, but have everlasting life.*

JOHN 3:16

Here is the most beloved verse in the Bible. What a
revelation of God, of Christ, of the depths and power
of love! How could He? Abraham gave his son, and God
graciously gave him back. But *God's Son*—the Son of
His love—the Only Begotten One—was given to a lost
world, to sinful men. How did He give Him? Clothed
in human form—a Man! Oh, the wonders of such a
love! How it should stir our hearts! How we should love
God for His gift! How we should love our Lord Jesus
Christ—God's Only Begotten Son!

*Let us with throbbing hearts for a lost world
go forth today, and all the days, to tell the
story to sinful, suffering men. Amen.*

---

187. THE GIFT OF GOD

*Jesus answered and said unto her, If thou knewest
the gift of God, and who it is that saith to thee,
Give me to drink; thou wouldest have asked of him,
and he would have given thee living water.*

JOHN 4:10

Here is that wonderful scene at the well of Samaria. The
Lord has gone out of His way to meet the poor, sinful

woman who has come to the well at a time when other women would not come; heavy-hearted, hopeless, but *One* loved her with a holy love. He is there and reveals Himself as the "*Gift of God.*" He is God's gift to us. What is our gift to Him? May we yield ourselves, and all we are and have to Him!

May we imitate the Samaritan woman and go forth with the message: Come, see a Man—God's Gift. Amen.

---

188. MESSIAH

The woman saith unto him, I know that Messias cometh, which is called Christ: when he is come, he will tell us all things.

JOHN 4:25

There is no book like the Bible and there never can be. Christ's interview with the woman at the well and His revelation of Himself is unique and contrary to any conception that could have been made of Him. The Samaritans, as did the Jews, anticipated a Christ (an Anointed One). This was the promise given in Deuteronomy 18:18. This woman was the last one we would have chosen for such a revelation—but her soul was filled at once with the Spirit of life and hope, and her lips bore a testimony—humiliating to herself—but bringing salvation to a multitude. Oh, that our lips might bear such convincing, convicting, and converting testimony.

Lord, make us like this Samaritan woman! Amen.

189. THE CHRIST, THE SAVIOUR OF THE WORLD

*We have heard him ourselves, and know that
this is indeed the Christ, the Saviour of the world.*

John 4:42

The testimony of one woman brings forth from the lips of many this title, "Christ, the Saviour of the world." For a two days' revival, Christ tarried in the little city of the Samaritans and there was a blessed first fruitage to His glory. These people, unlike the Jews, asked for no signs, no miracles. They took Him at His word, just as we must do. When He speaks, it is God that speaks. "We have heard him ourselves." The need of the world today is the personal experience of believers manifested in a personal devotion to Christ and in personal testimony to a hungry-hearted world.

*Oh, Thou Christ, Saviour of the world,
baptize us with the Spirit of service for Thee! Amen.*

---

190. THE TRUE BREAD FROM HEAVEN

My Father giveth you the true bread from heaven.

John 6:32

There had been a wonderful scene on the lakeside. A great multitude of people had wound their way around the lake to meet Jesus, and after a day of preaching, they were hungry and had no food. A little lad was used of God to bring about a great miracle. Five thousand men—beside the women and children—were fed and twelve baskets of fragments gathered. Moses, by God's power, brought daily bread from Heaven, but it was only temporal. Jesus is the *True* Bread from Heaven which, if men partake of, they live forever. He only can satisfy our soul's hunger. The world is starving for the True Bread.

*Lord Jesus, help us to go forth today
and feed some hungry souls. Amen.*

---

191. THE BREAD OF GOD

*For the bread of God is he which cometh down
from heaven, and giveth life unto the world.*
JOHN 6:33

In this verse Jesus reveals Himself as coming down from Heaven. The Bread of God is a gift to hungry humanity—a Divine gift—a Heavenly gift—a gift from God—a gift, spiritual and supernatural. Teachers, preachers, and workers for the Lord must always bear this in mind: The unsaved are hungry. Nothing will ever satisfy their hunger but the Bread of God—Jesus Christ. "He satisfieth the longing soul and filleth the hungry soul with goodness (God-Likeness)."

*Help us, Lord, to hear the cry of the hungry
souls all about us, and help us to minister
to them, in Thy name. Amen.*

192. THE BREAD OF LIFE

And Jesus said unto them, I am the bread of life:
he that cometh to me shall never hunger;
and he that believeth on me shall never thirst.

JOHN 6:35

Answering humanity's cry as embodied in the request, "Lord, evermore give us this bread," Jesus says: "I am the Bread of Life," i.e., the Life-eternal-giving Bread. This reply settles the question forever. He is the *true Bread,* the *Bread of God* and the *Bread of Life.* How is this Bread to be dispensed? It must be made known to an ignorant world. The terms upon which it is to be received must be made clear and definite. "Come to Me," says Jesus, "and you shall never hunger. Believe in Me and you shall never thirst." How simple! The "life gift" is a *love* gift. Never put a straw in the way of a hungry sinner. There is nothing to do but to believe—receive—accept. *Nothing more.*

Lord, help us to go out laden with the Bread
of Life and give it to the hungry. Amen.

---

193. THE LIVING BREAD

I am the living bread which came down from heaven.

JOHN 6:51

Here is the fourth assertion of our Lord concerning Himself as the "Bread of Heaven," the "True Bread," "Bread of God," "Bread of Life," and now "Living Bread." And He tells us that He will lay down His own life in order that we may have this Living Bread to eat and so live forever. The process by which we are to nourish the new nature which we received by accepting Him is by feeding on Him. If our bodies do not assimilate food they perish, and in the proportion that we do assimilate our food, we are able-bodied. Here is a searching lesson: Many believers are not strong. Paul says, "For this cause many are weak and sickly among you and many sleep."

Lord, make us strong through feeding upon Thyself. Amen.

---

194. THE LIGHT OF THE WORLD

Then spake Jesus again unto them, saying, I am the light of the world: he that followeth me shall not walk in darkness, but shall have the light of life.

JOHN 8:12

And God said, "Let there be light; and there was light." And "God divided the light from the darkness." Now our Lord says, "I am the Light of the World." The world is a dark, gloomy place, but "God is Light and in him is no darkness at all." If we follow Him we shall not walk in darkness. "Walking in the light," we have fellowship with one another and reflect the glory of His person in the gloom of the world. "Arise, shine, for thy light is come and the glory of the Lord is risen upon thee." He can only be manifested through the lives of His own and the light of the Word.

*O, Lord of Light, shine in our hearts
and through our lives. Amen.*

195. I AM

Jesus said unto them, Verily, verily, I say
unto you, Before Abraham was, I am.

John 8:58

The life of Abraham was limited. We know the time of his birth and of his departure. But there is no time limit to the life of our Lord. "Before Abraham was, I am." He was the Eternal Son of God. He was the Uncreated One, the Eternal One, the Self-existent One. Before the creation of the world He was the "I Am"! After the world passes away He will still be the "I Am." Without Him nothing was made that was made. He was God! Wonder of wonders! God manifest in the flesh! God pleading with men! God on the cross! God in the glory and coming in the clouds! Great, great is the mystery of God!

Son of God, Son of man, at the right hand of the
Glory, we bow in Thy presence and say with deepest
reverence, "Hallowed be Thy name." Amen.

---

196. THE DOOR OF THE SHEEP

Then said Jesus unto them again, Verily, verily,
I say unto you, I am the door of the sheep.

John 10:7

What contrast could be greater than that between the "I Am" and this title, "Door of the sheep"? Here our Lord paints a picture and uses an allegory into which sheep, sheepfold, and shepherd are introduced, He, Himself, claiming a peculiar position, "The Door of the sheep." He is the door by which entrance is gained to Heaven. "By me if any man enter in, he shall be saved." Put your hand upon the door—Jesus Christ on the cross—and enter the fold. There is safety. There is liberty. There is food for the sheep, and water and rest. Free from Satan's snare, filled with joy and peace, what more could we ask or desire?

Dear Lord, shepherd us today in Thine own arms. Amen.

---

197. THE GOOD SHEPHERD

I am the good shepherd: the good
shepherd giveth his life for the sheep.
JOHN 10:11

We shall have several meditations on our Lord as Shepherd, but here He speaks of Himself as the "*Good* Shepherd." God is good and Jesus is God. Therefore, He is good. If we could stop for a few moments and sense His presence, longing to speak to us in tones of deepest love, with His wonderful eyes fixed upon us, and His holy desire to draw us in loving tenderness to Himself— would we not say of Him, "He is so good. He died for me." And would not our hearts go out in passionate love to Him?

Loving Shepherd, help us to keep
close to Thee today. Amen.

198. ONE SHEPHERD

And other sheep I have, which are not of this fold:
them also I must bring, and they shall hear my voice;
and there shall be one fold, and one shepherd.

John 10:16

Israel had a limited view of our Christ. They were wrapped up in themselves. Selfish, narrow in their vision of the Messiah that was to come, they were without compassion, as we ourselves so often are, having no patience with those who differ from us. Not so our Lord. He had a heart boundless in love; a soul longing for the children of men; looking forward into the future, seeing the hatred of the Jews (His own people) to the cross, the cruel death, and then the many sheep, washed in the same blood, filled with the same Holy Spirit of Life, folded in the *one fold*. Wonderful vision!

Shepherd of our lives, enlarge our hearts in sympathy with
the pulsings of Thine Own loving heart. Amen.

---

199. THE RESURRECTION

Jesus said unto her, I am the resurrection, and the life: he
that believeth in me, though he were dead, yet shall he live.

John 11:25

Here our Lord links His own title "I Am" with the resurrection, "I am the gift of the resurrection to all who believe on Me. Though he die, who believeth on Me, yet shall he live." Faith in Him equals eternal life and that assures our resurrection. Because He lives, we *must* live. Death may come to us, but it will be the shadow only, which will pass and leave us in the full sunlight of eternal life. Nothing can separate us. He who raised up Christ from the dead shall quicken our bodies. "Whosoever liveth and believeth in Me, shall never die." In His resurrection He conquered death. Praise the Lord!

Lord Jesus, come quickly and change these
bodies of our abasement into the likeness
of Thine own glorified body. Amen.

---

200. THE CHRIST, THE SON OF GOD

She saith unto him, Yea, Lord: I believe
that thou art the Christ, the Son of God.
JOHN 11:27

Here is a remarkable confession from the lips of Martha, "The Christ, the Son of God." Lazarus was in the tomb. Her eyes, no doubt, were full of tears, her soul full of sorrow, but her faith in Jesus as the Christ never wavered. She heard that Jesus was coming and called Him "Lord"; then she said, "I believe that Thou art the Christ, the Son of God." How sweet! How blessed! but yet the heart of Jesus was pained, for He groaned in spirit because of her lack of faith that He would answer prayer and raise Lazarus up.

Lord Jesus, help us never to disappoint Thee in our faith in
Thy power and Thy promise to answer our faith. Amen.

201. A GRAIN OF WHEAT

And Jesus answered them, saying, The hour is come,
that the Son of man should be glorified. Verily,
verily, I say unto you, Except a corn [grain] of wheat
fall into the ground and die, it abideth alone:
but if it die, it bringeth forth much fruit.

JOHN 12:23–24

Before He could be glorified He must be as a grain of
wheat. How insignificant seems a grain of wheat, and yet
this suggestion is one of the most wonderful in the Word
of God. A grain of wheat is so small that it can hardly
be held between the fingers without dropping, and yet
it is associated with *His glory*. He must die in order to
bring forth fruit. So must we, if we are to be like Him.
How hard it seems to human pride to become as a grain
of wheat and then to die to this world. But listen to the
words of His testimony and look upon His example. Do
we desire to be like Him?

Lord, help us to ponder upon this truth
today and long to be more like Thee. Amen.

---

202. MASTER

Ye call me Master and Lord: and ye say well; for so I am.

JOHN 13:13

"Master" means "Teacher" and the authoritative Teacher
He was and is. We are to learn of Him, for He is the
Truth and reveals the truth to men. He has left to us His

words of wisdom and we are to sit at His feet and learn of Him. We recognize this position of our Lord by yielding submission to His authority and acknowledging it daily. He knows the past. He knows the present. He knows the future. Let our prayer be,

Lord, teach us Thy will, through Thy Word. Help us to know, understand, and gladly live out Thy will. Amen.

---

203. THE WAY

Jesus saith unto him, I am the way.
JOHN 14:6

He is the Way—"a Way without deviation"—the strait and narrow Way, the only Way which leads directly to the Father. There are a thousand ways which lead to destruction, to eternal darkness and separation from the Father. Satan has multiplied agents pointing to his wicked way, but Christ is the Sign Post, saying: "This is the Way; walk ye in it." When we walk in *the Way* we walk in the light. We journey with Himself in sweet fellowship. What a joyful journey! The Way is lightened by His countenance. He holds us by the hand. He supplies our needs. What a Saviour!

Lord, help us to keep in touch with Thee as we travel along the Heavenly highway to the home prepared for us by Thee. Amen.

204. THE TRUTH

Jesus saith unto him, I am. . .the truth.
JOHN 14:6

He is not only the Way, but He is the *Truth*—"the truth without any contradiction." We are God's free men, for we know Him who is the Truth, and the Truth makes us free. He is the Truth about the Word of God. Hear Him say, "I am not come to destroy the law or the prophets, but to fulfill." And "It is easier for Heaven and earth to pass than for one jot or tittle of the law to fail." Pity the poor deceived students in the schools and the devil-deluded ministers and teachers who cast any reflection upon the Word of God to which Jesus has set His eternal seal! Doubt concerning the inerrancy of the Bible is a doubt concerning Himself. Do not taint your soul with such unholy thoughts.

Lord, Thou art the Truth. We look to Thee.
Guide us into the Truth all the days. Amen.

---

205. THE LIFE

Jesus saith unto him, I am. . .the life.
JOHN 14:6

He is not only the Way and the Truth, but He is the Life—Eternal Life, the Author of Life, and the Giver of Life. We almost stagger when we confront this statement by the One who left Heaven and the throne of God and came to this earth that He might reveal Himself and receive to Himself those who were to inherit through Him and share with Him this eternal Life. Our short pilgrimage here is soon ended and then, O joy, we enter the unending, eternal Life.

Lord, how we thank Thee that Thou art our eternal
Life through the indwelling Holy Spirit. Amen.

---

206. THE VINE

I am the vine, ye are the branches: He that abideth
in me, and I in him, the same bringeth forth much
fruit: for without me ye can do nothing.
JOHN 15:5

Here the Lord calls Himself "The Vine" as He associates Himself with the branches. He is the root and stem upon which we, as branches, must depend. The purpose of the Vine is to bear fruit. The life is in the *vine*, but that life is also in the branches, and we are to be fruit-bearing branches. "He that *abideth* in Me and I in him, the same bringeth forth much fruit." We can bear no fruit of ourselves. Our dependence is upon Him. The desire of the Husbandman is to produce fruit, and we must ask ourselves the question: "Am I a fruit-bearing branch? If not, why not?" How patient He is, yet how fearful is the contemplation of the thought: "I may be a fruitless branch."

Lord, forbid that it should be so. Holy Spirit, fill us
with Thyself that we may bear much fruit. Amen.

207. THE OVERCOMER

I have overcome the world.

John 16:33

A graphic picture—one of the "last night messages" of our Lord—fraught with tremendous interest to every believer. A world of tribulation confronted Him, and a world of tribulation confronts His church. "Ye shall have tribulation" and we do, but in Him we have peace— the peace of God, which passeth understanding. How blessed to be in Him who is the Source of our strength! We must learn to overcome through Him. There is nothing too hard for Him. He loves to give us victory. We please Him by trusting Him and taking by faith what He has purchased for us.

Let us bow in His presence and commit all to Him for victory today and thus glorify our Overcomer. Amen.

---

208. OUR KEEPER

While I was with them in the world, I kept them in thy name: those that thou gavest me I have kept.

John 17:12

This prayer on the night before His crucifixion is one of sacred sweetness and comfort. While He was here He guarded and kept His own. Now He is in the glory and still guards and keeps us. The enemy, Satan, who captured and controlled Judas, would separate us, if he could, from our Lord; but He is our Keeper and we can trust in His unfailing promise: "I will him keep in perfect peace whose mind is stayed on Me because he trusteth in Me." The enemy has ten thousand agents seeking to spoil our lives, but nothing can separate us from the love of God as manifested in Christ Jesus our Lord.

"Now unto Him who is able to keep us from falling. . .to the only wise God, our Saviour, be glory, forever." Amen.

---

209. THE SENT OF THE FATHER

As thou hast sent me into the world,
even so have I also sent them into the world.
JOHN 17:18

From the glory which He had with the Father before the world was, He was sent into this world of sin and shame to redeem sinful men. He was God's Apostle—God's "Sent One." His prayer now to the Father is that they might be *sanctified* (set apart) as He was set apart for the work of redemption. He prays that His disciples might also be set apart for the great work of saving men. Christ has not changed. This prayer was for us, also, as He says in verse 20: "Neither pray I for these alone, but for them also which shall believe on me through their word." His holy desire is that we might be in the world with the same message that He Himself had.

Lord Jesus, help us to recognize today
Thy call and our calling to save souls. Amen.

210. THE MAN

Behold the man!
JOHN 19:5

"Behold the Man!" How little Pilate knew what he was doing when he bestowed upon our Lord that significant title, "The Man!" The word "man" is used nearly three thousand times in the Bible, but there is only one "THE MAN"—the Man from Heaven. The word in the original is "Adam"—a human being—and such He was. Oh, the marvel of it! It seems too good to be true, and yet it is true. For our sakes—in order to be one with us and to bear our sin—He threw aside His royal vesture and donned the garments of humanity, that He might interpret to us the purpose of the Father.

In the name of this Man, our Father, we ask for guidance today and pray that our hearts may be in tune with His. Amen.

---

211. MY LORD AND MY GOD

And Thomas answered and said unto him, My LORD and my God.
JOHN 20:28

Thomas is the doubting disciple. He loved His Lord and had been willing to die with Him, but could not believe in His bodily resurrection. He demanded a definite proof. Eight days had passed when he is confronted with the risen Jesus who says, "Put your finger in my hands, and put your hand in My side; and be not faithless but believing," and out of a heart throbbing with joy Thomas cries, "My Lord and my God." How sympathetically loving is our Lord with our unbelief. How patient He is, yet how He longs for our unquestioning, implicit faith. Let us honor Him by believing Him with all our heart.

Our Lord and our God, help us today to look upon the wounds which Thou carriest for us and with full faith renew our pledge of loyalty to Thee. Amen.

---

212. A MAN APPROVED OF GOD

Jesus of Nazareth, a man approved of God among you by miracles and wonders and signs, which God did by him in the midst of you.
ACTS 2:22

This is the testimony of Peter, the fisherman-apostle, concerning our Lord, Jesus of Nazareth. "A man approved of God!" He professed to be the promised Messiah, the Son of God, and made good His profession by His public life. His miraculous works were the proof of miraculous power. He was God in human form. He set His followers the example for holy living. When believers are anointed of the Holy Spirit and seek by lip and life to honor their Lord, the approval of God the Father will be upon them.

Lord, help us to live a life approved of God, so that through us wonders may be wrought in the salvation of souls. Amen.

213. THINE HOLY ONE

Because thou wilt not leave my soul in hell, neither wilt thou suffer thine Holy One to see corruption.

ACTS 2:27

The Godhead and manhood were united in Christ, and it was impossible that He should be holden by the power of death. He passed through the agony; He paid the penalty; He suffered the separation; but death could not hold Him. The unfailing Word of God had promised His resurrection and so "up from the grave He arose." He hath broken the bars of death from us and in the freedom of the new life, with glorified bodies, we will be forever with Him.

May our souls be led to magnify Thee, the Holy One, this day and rejoice in the hope of soon being with Thee. Amen.

---

214. THE HOLY ONE AND JUST

But ye denied the Holy One and the Just, and desired a murderer to be granted unto you.

ACTS 3:14

Peter is delivering a sermon to the Jews. They had looked with wonder at the lame man healed by the hand of Peter, and Peter was taking advantage of the opportunity to set before them the resurrected Christ as the One whom they had condemned but whom God had raised from the dead, to whom he gives this title "Holy One and Just." And such is He, the Spotless One, without sin,

God manifest in the flesh. Do we recognize Him as the Holy One? Sometimes familiarity breeds indifference. May it never be so with us. Every suggestion of "the Holy One" should stir our souls in adoration and holy desire to be like Him.

Oh, Thou Holy One, may we seek earnestly this day to live as in Thy sight, adoring Thee constantly. Amen.

215. THE PRINCE OF LIFE

And killed the Prince of life, whom God hath raised from the dead; whereof we are witnesses.
ACTS 3:15

"The Prince of Life"—a remarkable title to give to our Lord when viewed in contrast with Barabbas, the murderer who took life. One—the bestower of life; the other—the destroyer of life. He came that men might have life and life more abundantly. How many there are who ignore and reject Him who will never have the joy of living and reigning with Him through the eternal ages. Are we doing our best to make Him known to lost men?

Lord Jesus, Thou Prince of Life, stir our hearts with compassion for the lost, and help us today to make Thee known to some blinded soul. Amen.

216. THE HOLY CHILD JESUS

For of a truth against thy holy child Jesus, whom thou hast anointed, both Herod, and Pontius Pilate, with the Gentiles, and the people of Israel, were gathered together.
ACTS 4:27

Peter and John are before the Council to be examined in connection with the miracle of the healing of the lame man. They gave their testimony to the fact that it was in the despised name of Jesus Christ of Nazareth that this had been done. The Council could do naught but let them go. They went at once to the place where the church were gathered together and reported what had been done and the assembly lifted their voices in thanksgiving, glorifying the name of the "Holy Child Jesus" against whom His enemies were gathered. They prayed that in the name of this Holy Child Jesus signs and wonders might be wrought and they were.

Lord Jesus, we thank Thee that they are being wrought today and will be until Thou dost come again. Amen.

---

217. A PRINCE AND A SAVIOUR

Him hath God exalted with his right hand to be a Prince and a Saviour.
ACTS 5:31

Here is a picture and a theme for our meditation. A convict—a criminal in the sight of men—hanging on a tree, dying an awful death of shame, suffering the agonies of hell itself that the question of sinful man's sin might be settled forever—exalted by God to the highest heights—a Prince! But to establish His title He became the Sin-bearer that He might become the Sin-blotter. Destined to deepest depths of human suffering and humility, but raised to the highest heights of honor and glory. Oh, the wretchedness of our sin which demanded it, and the wonders of a Saviour which delivered it!

Lord Jesus, our Prince and our Saviour,
we yield ourselves to Thee with glad hearts. Amen.

---

218. THE JUST ONE

Which of the prophets have not your fathers persecuted? and they have slain them which shewed before of the coming of the Just One; of whom ye have been now the betrayers and murderers.

ACTS 7:52

The words "Just (righteous) One" burst from the lips of Stephen, the first martyr, in the wonderful message which he gave before the Council in defending the name and glory of our Lord Jesus Christ. He paid with his life for his loyalty to his Lord and will receive his reward. It was through his testimony that the Spirit of God brought conviction to Saul of Tarsus, resulting in his conversion. How much would *we* be willing to suffer for Him?

Oh, Thou blessed Saviour of our souls, warm
our hearts in devotion to Thee. Make us sturdy
and strong as defenders of the faith. Amen.

219. LORD JESUS

And they stoned Stephen, calling upon God,
and saying, Lord Jesus, receive my spirit.
ACTS 7:59

Stephen is passing through the fire of Jewish hatred. But God is faithful to His faithful servant and martyr and opens the Heavens to him showing him Jesus standing at the right of His glory. The cry of Stephen was "Lord Jesus, receive my spirit." His prayer was like that of Jesus who said, "Father, into Thy hands I commend My spirit" (Luke 23:46). What a testimony to the Deity of our Lord! Only He who gave the spirit could receive it. To depart and be with Christ was far better for Stephen and it will be for us when in His own good time He calls us.

Lord Jesus, help us to witness a good confession, gladly
facing any foe, even death that, like Stephen, we may
glorify Thee whether in life or death. Amen.

---

220. LORD OF ALL

The word which God sent unto the children of Israel,
preaching peace by Jesus Christ: (he is Lord of all).
ACTS 10:36

Jesus Christ is Lord of all men. Peter was a Jew and did not want to depart from Jewish ground, but God sent him a vision from Heaven to make clear to him that He was no respecter of persons. "While Peter yet spoke the Holy Ghost fell upon all that heard the Word." Our Lord loves all; He died for all; He commissions us to go and preach to all. The world is the field, and every soul living has a claim upon us, which we must meet and answer for. What a wonderful Lord of all! What a wonderful Gospel! What a wonderful salvation!

Oh, Thou Lord of all, reprove us today for our selfishness, our lack of likeness to Thee, and fill us with the Holy Ghost that we may gladly be witnesses to all men. Amen.

221. THE JUDGE OF QUICK AND DEAD

And he commanded us to preach unto the people, and to testify that it is he which was ordained of God to be the Judge of quick and dead.

ACTS 10:42

Here is a testimony to the fact of the resurrection of the dead and a judgment of the living and the dead of all generations. Christ's position is one of dignity and power and must be recognized. In love for men, He became a Man, mingled with men, manifested His love for individuals as well as for all men—but it must not be forgotten that He is also the *Judge* of all men. Believers have rights and titles conferred upon them by reason of their acceptance of the sacrifice of Jesus Christ, but they, too, must face Him to be judged for their works. *The Day* must come and we must face it.

Lord, we are Thine and Thou art ours. Let us adore and serve Thee today. Amen.

222. THAT MAN WHOM HE HATH ORDAINED

Because he hath appointed a day, in the which he will judge the world in righteousness by that man whom he hath ordained.

ACTS 17:31

Jesus was ordained—set apart—appointed—designated—as THE MAN who is to judge the whole human race, and the evidence, or proof, of this is the fact of His resurrection from the dead. It will be a righteous judgment by a righteous Judge. It will be an impartial judgment by One who created all things, and who knows all things, a holy, unerring Judge. He will have the books opened before Him, and there can never be any appeal from the verdict. What is your relation to this Ordained Man? Are you ready?

Lord, help us to be faithful witnesses while it is called today. Amen.

---

223. JESUS OF NAZARETH

And I answered, Who art thou, Lord? And he said unto me, I am Jesus of Nazareth, whom thou persecutest.

ACTS 22:8

More than twenty times in the Scriptures is our Lord called "Jesus of Nazareth." Here it is remarkable. Paul is telling the story of his conversion. He is bound with chains, a prisoner, in the hands of the Roman authorities.

He says that the words which came to him from the Heavens were "Saul, Saul, why persecutest thou Me?" And in answer to his question, "Who art thou, Lord?" came the answer, "I am Jesus of Nazareth." That is His name now. From the glory He acknowledges His earthly title—"Jesus of Nazareth." Jesus is God. He made the worlds, but He acknowledges the little obscure town of Nazareth, His "hometown" down here.

Jesus of Nazareth, we want to be one with Thee. Guide us to Thy glory. Amen.

224. JESUS CHRIST OUR LORD

*That as sin hath reigned unto death,
even so might grace reign through righteousness
unto eternal life by Jesus Christ our Lord.*

ROMANS 5:21

Here we have the grouping of three titles, "Jesus" (Saviour) "Christ" (Anointed) "Lord" (Master). In a few words the great problem of the ages is solved. Sin, with its death-dealing power, wore the crown of victory over mortal man, but there was One greater than Satan, the author of sin, and in that One was manifested the victorious power of grace (unmerited favor) by which, through the sacrifice of Jesus Christ, God's condescending love could be manifested in His Son, our Lord and Master.

"Jesus Christ, our Lord"—we breathe the words with joyful lips and give Thee thanks for that grace which has saved and which keeps us. Amen.

---

225. THE FIRST-BORN AMONG MANY BRETHREN

For whom he did foreknow, he also did predestinate to be conformed to the image of his Son, that he might be the firstborn among many brethren.

ROMANS 8:29

A wonderful title for our Lord, "The First-Born"! Adam was the first-born among men, but he forfeited his rights and privileges through sin and God ordained another Man to be the First, who was to be born of a woman and be the Head of a great company of brethren. God has plans for the human race and is carrying them out as the years come and go. Jesus is the "*First*-born" and we who are "born-again" ones are, by His grace, being conformed to His image, and, when He comes from Heaven, we will be among the sons of God and united forever to and with Him.

Our eyes are fastened upon Thee, Thou First-Born One, today, and we say out of our hearts, come quickly. Amen.

226. HIS OWN SON

He that spared not his own Son, but delivered
him up for us all, how shall he not with
him also freely give us all things?
ROMANS 8:32

"His Own Son," "His Only Son," "The Son of His Love"—the dearest, the best He gave, out of His great heart freely, lovingly, once for all to the sinful children of men. Having given us His best, will He withhold anything from us? Why do we doubt Him? Why do we live such poor, selfish, sordid lives, when the world is so needy, when hearts are so heavy and broken? Why do we fail to appropriate what He has so freely offered us? Is there not a challenge to us here? Let us meet it today.

Lord, help us to believe and with joyful hearts ask for great
things for a needy world in the name of Thy Son. Amen.

---

227. GOD BLESSED FOREVER

Whose are the fathers, and of whom as concerning the flesh
Christ came, who is over all, God blessed for ever. Amen.
ROMANS 9:5

As we journey through the Word of God how Christ illumines it all with His presence! His titles are many. How significant is this "God blessed forever"! The promised Messiah of the Jewish stock and the flower of its race, yet they would not receive Him. He was the Shekinah glory tabernacling in human form in the midst of the world. But their eyes were blinded, and what centuries of sorrow have followed and will follow until He comes for His own, and then will come the saddest of all experiences for them. Pity both Jew and Gentile in our own day who refuse to acknowledge Him as "God blessed forever."

May we bow to Him today and say from our hearts, "To us Thou art indeed 'God blessed forever.'" Amen.

---

228. LORD OVER ALL

For there is no difference between the Jew and the Greek: for the same Lord over all is rich unto all that call upon him.

ROMANS 10:12

"He is rich unto all who call upon him." Then why not call? The only requirement is that we belong to His family. The door is open to all to join that family, and for the family there are riches of revelation, riches of forgiveness, riches of grace, riches of love. Just call in His name, and He will answer, for "Whatsoever ye shall ask the Father in My name, that will I do," and that word "whatsoever" comprehends everything. He will supply *all* your need. How much we lose—how much we lose, because we do not call.

Lord, over all, hear our prayer today. May we glory in the riches of Thy name, and wilt Thou incline us to believe and receive. Amen.

229. THE LORD

For whosoever shall call upon the
name of the Lord shall be saved.

ROMANS 10:13

The Master loves to hear the call of a sinner for salvation. How many sin-sick, weary souls there are who are hungry for salvation. They do not know this verse. They have false ideas about Christ and about salvation. They would gladly cry to the Lord but He has not been revealed to them. They need someone to tell them of His longing to have them in His family. "Faith cometh by hearing and hearing by the Word of God." Listen to the words, "How beautiful are the feet of them that preach the Gospel of peace and bring glad tidings of good things." "To preach" means "to tell out," "to proclaim"—and if you are a believer then you are a God-ordained preacher and will be held accountable for your ministry.

Oh, Lord, our Master, send us all out
today to tell the love story to others. Amen.

---

230. THE DELIVERER

And so all Israel shall be saved: as it is written,
There shall come out of Sion the Deliverer,
and shall turn away ungodliness from Jacob.

ROMANS 11:26

Here we face a startling prophecy. The ancient people of God, scattered about in every land without a country of their own save as certain permission is given them—as now to reside in the old land—these Jews are yet to be delivered and as a nation they shall turn to Christ as their Deliverer and shall be God's earthly people as we shall be His Heavenly people. Let us never forget how much we owe to the Jewish race and let us seek earnestly to bring as many as possible of them to Christ now.

Oh, Lord Jesus, Thou hast been our Deliverer. We glory in Thy name. Help us to help others to know Thee. Amen.

---

231. LORD BOTH OF THE DEAD AND THE LIVING

For to this end Christ both died, and rose, and revived, that he might be Lord both of the dead and living.
ROMANS 14:9

Christ is the center of all affairs as related to this earth. He rules. He reigns. He keeps books and some day those books are to be opened. Adam and Eve and everyone that has ever lived will be there to answer to the call. Saints (or saved ones) will be judged for their manner of living. That will be one judgment. Sinners will be judged, and that will be another judgment. There can be no evasions, no exceptions. All accounts must be faced and settled. Men should live in that prospect. How blessed for those whose sins are covered by the blood! But how sorrowful for even those if they have not sought to do their best for Him!

Oh, Lord, may the words of our mouths and the thoughts of our hearts be pleasing to Thee this day. Amen.

---

232. MINISTER OF THE CIRCUMCISION

Now I say that Jesus Christ was a minister of the circumcision for the truth of God, to confirm the promises made unto the fathers.

ROMANS 15:8

Here again we have a title which unites in the Spirit both Jew and Gentile as partakers of the grace of God. He came to the Jews with His message of love, but they would not have Him. He turned to the Gentiles and some received Him. The gospel of Jesus Christ is for all men, because all have sinned. He came for all. He loved all. He died for all. He longs to gather all unto Himself. He is the "Minister of the Circumcision" and the "Minister of the Cross." We are one in Him.

Oh, Thou blessed One, minister unto us today and help us to minister unto Thee. Amen.

---

233. THE POWER OF GOD

But unto them which are called, both Jews and Greeks, Christ the power of God.

1 CORINTHIANS 1:24

When we use the word "power," we are possessed with a strange sensation. Every fibre of our beings is tense and we think of might and authority. So when we think of our Lord Jesus Christ we can visualize Him as the Mighty One. From a power-house the electric current issues and darkness is displaced by light; the engine is imbued with life and moves the train carrying, perchance, the armies of a nation. So our Lord Jesus Christ is the Power of God, for all power is committed unto Him. He speaks and it is done! And this Powerful One has said, "Ask and ye shall receive." How wonderful that He should love such as we!

Lord Jesus, we commend ourselves to Thee today and rest in faith in the power of Thy love for us. Amen.

---

234. THE WISDOM OF GOD

But unto them which are called, both Jews and Greeks, Christ. . .the wisdom of God.
1 CORINTHIANS 1:24

To those who are called He is the Wisdom of God. The Bible teaches us that wisdom is the principal thing and, therefore, we should seek wisdom and Him who is the storehouse of wisdom. "Never man spake like this Man." "If any man lack wisdom, let him ask in faith, nothing wavering." "Giving doth not impoverish him." "The wisdom of the world is foolishness with Him." Then let us be wise and seek the wisdom that passeth all understanding.

Lord, as we face the duties and privileges of this day, guide us by Thy wisdom to Thy praise and glory. Amen.

235. RIGHTEOUSNESS

But of him are ye in Christ Jesus, who of
God is made unto us. . .righteousness.

1 CORINTHIANS 1:30

Righteousness is "rightness." We were all wrong and always wrong, but in Him we are made right. All of our righteousness was as filthy rags. There was nothing in us that would commend us to God and never could be. But what a change when we are in Him and He is in us. We are made sinless, *in Him*, for He bore all our sins and paid all the penalty, and His righteousness is imputed to us. What a joy to be *consciously* in Him! And what a price He paid in order to become our righteousness!

Lord, teach us to recognize this day our unworthiness
and to dwell much upon the fact that THOU
ART OUR RIGHTEOUSNESS. *Amen.*

---

236. SANCTIFICATION

But of him are ye in Christ Jesus, who of
God is made unto us. . .sanctification.

1 CORINTHIANS 1:30

To be "sanctified" is to be "separated"—"set apart." We could never be sanctified by our own efforts, for we are absolutely helpless save as Thou dost become all things to us. We are in Christ Jesus and what He is, we are, and what He has, we share. We are nothing. Thou art everything. Help us to see ourselves in Christ Jesus. Thou hast set us apart to be Thy representatives in a lost world. In every act and deed we represent Thee.

Lord, today, may the words of our mouths and the meditations of our hearts, be acceptable unto Thee. Amen.

---

237. REDEMPTION

But of him are ye in Christ Jesus, who of God is made unto us. . .redemption.
1 CORINTHIANS 1:30

What an awful thing is sin, and "coming short of the glory of God" is sin. How can any sensible person ever conceive of the possibility of a soul living with God with a sinful nature? The grace of God is wonderful. He loved us. He gave His Son for our redemption, and that Son poured out His life blood to atone for our sins. Who could measure the height or depth, or length or breadth of such love? Shall we not manifest our love by yielding all that we are and have to Him?

Our blessed Lord, help us to walk in the light of Thy love this day as the redeemed of Thee. Amen.

---

238. THE LORD OF GLORY

Which none of the princes of this world knew: for had they known it, they would not have crucified the Lord of glory.
1 CORINTHIANS 2:8

What a title is this! Back of it are the eternal years which the mind of man can never penetrate. "The Lord of Glory"—Creator of all things, in whom is wrapped up all wisdom and power. "Had they known!" Oh, the pity of it that eyes are closed and hearts bolted against the revelation of our Lord who descended from the heights of glory and went into the depths of human sorrow and suffering in order to reveal Himself to sinful men. Pity the poor princes of this world who resist the entreaties of the Holy Spirit to receive Him as Saviour and Lord.

Oh, Thou gracious Lord, make our meditations
of Thee sweet this day. Amen.

---

239. THE FOUNDATION

For other foundation can no man lay
than that is laid, which is Jesus Christ.
1 CORINTHIANS 3:11

Here we have a wonderful title for our Lord—"Jesus Christ, the Foundation." That foundation was laid before the world was created. There is no other. Upon this Foundation is built all of the purposes of God for time and for eternity. Upon it is being built the church, "a holy temple," and a "habitation of God through the Spirit." How is this structure to be built? By the Holy Spirit through His own beloved disciples who are endued and endowed with power to go into the world and gather the stones of human souls. What a wonderful work is assigned to us, working in harmony with Himself.

*Dear Lord, be with us this day as we seek to
gather to Thyself precious souls who shall
become stones in Thy temple. Amen.*

---

240. OUR PASSOVER

*Purge out therefore the old leaven, that ye may
be a new lump, as ye are unleavened. For even
Christ our passover is sacrificed for us.*
1 CORINTHIANS 5:7

The Jews had their Passover which commemorated their
flight from Egypt which God accomplished with a high
hand and a stretched out arm. It was a foretaste of our
Passover—a Lamb without blemish, slain for our sins,
whose blood sprinkled upon our hearts cleanses from
sin, and whose broken body feeds our souls. With us it
is a *daily* feast. By it we are separated from the worldly
Egypt and safe forevermore. Therefore, let us keep the
feast with the unleavened bread of sincerity and truth.

*Lord Jesus, in fellowship sweet we would sit at
Thy feet and feast on Thee, this day. Amen.*

---

241. THAT SPIRITUAL ROCK

*And did all drink the same spiritual drink:
for they drank of that spiritual Rock that
followed them: and that Rock was Christ.*
1 CORINTHIANS 10:4

Paul is calling attention to the journey of the children of Israel through the wilderness and comparing it to the life of the church. They were supernaturally supplied daily with food and water. The water was a gift from God; symbolizing the Water of Life which springs from the spiritual Rock, which is Christ. He is our Rock, and from His riven side flow rivers of living water. How often we have sung, "Jesus the Water of Life will give, freely, freely, freely"—and then how often we have forgotten to slake our thirst from that Fountain which will never cease to flow down through the ages.

Lord Jesus, our spiritual Rock, help us to
drink freely of Thy living water today. Amen.

---

242. THE HEAD OF EVERY MAN

But I would have you know,
that the head of every man is Christ.
1 CORINTHIANS 11:3

God reigns supreme in this world, but God is manifested in the flesh in the person of Jesus, who is supreme over all humanity, and every man is morally bound to acknowledge and obey His authority. He is the "Head over all things to the church." Were the church to acknowledge His authority and become obedient to His command, what a different condition would exist. As Head of the church He has given orders to "Go into all the world and preach the Gospel," but, alas, His command has not been obeyed. Let us bow to His mandate and let every one of us seek to do our part.

*Lord Jesus, we bow to Thy mandate today. Help us
to tell the story of the cross to a lost world. Amen.*

---

243. THE FIRST-FRUITS
OF THEM THAT SLEEP

*But now is Christ risen from the dead,
and become the firstfruits of them that slept.*

1 CORINTHIANS 15:20

Here is an emphatic statement, "Now *is* Christ risen."
There can be no controversy over this fact. The church
itself is the challenge to all doubters. The Bible, the lives
of believers, all witness to the fact of His resurrection. He
is the *first-fruits*, and every believer looks forward with
glad anticipation to the coming day of all days when
the trumpet shall sound and "the dead in Christ shall
rise first." This is the blessed hope—to be with Him and
like Him forever.

*Make this a glad day, our Lord, as we contemplate
this wonderful truth and think of Thee as the
coming, glorious One. Amen.*

---

244. THE LAST ADAM

*And so it is written, The first man Adam was made a
living soul; the last Adam was made a quickening spirit.*

1 CORINTHIANS 15:45

The *first* Adam was created out of the dust of the earth

and God breathed into his nostrils the breath of life. The *last* Adam was conceived by the Holy Ghost. He was a "God-Man." The first Adam was innocent; the last Adam was holy. The first became a sinner; the second was sinless. He was a life-giving Spirit. He was the Life-giver and the Light-giver. Through this last Adam, through faith, we receive the nature which prepares us for an eternal inheritance and qualifies us for the celestial joys of the celestial city.

Our Lord, Thou hast quickened us by the indwelling Spirit, and we meditate with grateful hearts upon Thee, the last Adam. Amen.

---

245. THE LORD FROM HEAVEN

The first man is of the earth, earthy; the second man is the Lord from heaven.
1 CORINTHIANS 15:47

The contrast here again is between Adam and Christ. Adam was of the earth. The Lord was from Heaven. The first man was a failure and all men are born in sin and are failures. Therefore, the necessity of a "Man from Heaven." Our eyes are fixed upon Him today—this "Second Man." All men bear the image of the earthly, but to bear the image of the Heavenly, Christ should be their desire. Let us seek by holy fellowship with Him today to reflect His image in this sinful world.

Lord Jesus, help us to walk with Thee today. Amen.

246. A QUICKENING SPIRIT

And so it is written. . .the last Adam
was made a quickening spirit.
1 CORINTHIANS 15:45

We are of the earth, earthy, by birth, but we have a new birth. That which was first was natural and earthy; afterwards comes the spiritual. How wonderful is the operation of God in creating in fallen man an eternal life! "He that hath the Son hath life." These mortal bodies shall become, through the power of our Lord as the quickening Spirit, glorious, immortal bodies in which He will dwell throughout the eternal years. What a glorious outlook for us whose eyes are turned heavenward from whence we look for Him.

Oh, Thou quickening Spirit, come quickly!
We long to see Thee! Amen.

---

247. THE IMAGE OF GOD

In whom the god of this world hath blinded the
minds of them which believe not, lest the light
of the glorious gospel of Christ, who is the
image of God, should shine unto them.
2 CORINTHIANS 4:4

Satan is the god of this world and the prince of the power of the air. The eyes of every unsaved person have been blinded to the vision of Christ who is the *image of God.* Their minds are on earthly things in which there is no joy, no peace, no satisfaction. Satan hates our Lord with a bitter hatred, and as the days pass and the coming of the Lord draws near, Satan's blinding powers are more and more manifest. This fact should stir our hearts to increased desire and intensified purpose to present to the unsaved, Jesus, the Image of God, who is so precious to us.

Lord Jesus, fill us with Thy Holy Spirit and give us a passion for the blinded souls of the unsaved. Amen.

---

248. THE UNSPEAKABLE GIFT

Thanks be unto God for his unspeakable gift.
2 CORINTHIANS 9:15

Paul has been praising the Corinthians for their liberal gifts to the saints in Judea. His heart is full and he breaks forth in a note of praise as he thinks of God's greater gift of His Son—"Thanks. . .for the unspeakable Gift." There was no treasure which God could give comparable to the gift of His Son, and "Having given us his Son, will he not with him freely give us all things?" How could it be possible that the Father would give to sinners the Son of His Love? How we ought to love Him! Is there anything we have or are that we would withhold from Him?

Loving Lord, help us to sense in a new way what it means for us to possess Thee, the unspeakable Gift. Amen.

249. CHRIST

Blessed be the God and Father of our Lord Jesus
Christ, who hath blessed us with all spiritual
blessings in heavenly places in Christ.
EPHESIANS 1:3

Three times is the word "bless" used in this verse. God is a blessed God and He showers His blessings upon His people. What are the spiritual blessings in Christ? They are spiritual gifts, the blessing of the Gospel— the "good news" from God. They include the eternal purpose and precious promises of God which are to be manifested now, in the future, and throughout eternity. As you read your Bible, note them. How many! How strengthening! How encouraging! How satisfying! How enduring! And all *in* Christ and *only* in Him.

How we rejoice, oh, Thou Christ of God, that by faith
we are in Thee and all of Thy blessings are for us. Help
us to appropriate them with thankful hearts. Amen.

---

250. HEAD OVER ALL THINGS

And hath put all things under his feet, and gave
him to be the head over all things to the church.
EPHESIANS 1:22

The gift of God to the church—which is His body— was Christ, whom He raised from the dead and seated Him above all principalities and powers and might and dominion and every name which is named both in this world and in that which is to come. We need to recognize our exalted position—bone of His bone and flesh of His flesh—chosen in Him before the world was—dear as the apple of His eye. Let us live in the enjoyment of our great privileges and in the assurance that through the endless ages we shall be His blessed, beloved ones.

Oh, Thou Head of the church, keep us in happy, holy, heavenly fellowship with Thyself this day, and until Thou dost come! Amen.

---

251. HE THAT FILLETH ALL IN ALL

Which is his body, the fulness of him that filleth all in all.

EPHESIANS 1:23

The church is the "fullness of Christ." Christ could never be complete without the church and the church can never be complete until the last member is brought into the body. Therefore, the business of the church is to be busy seeking to save the lost. Every soul added increases His fullness. The life of Christ pulses through His body, the church, and through each individual member. Why, then, are we not filled with Christ? Because we are not yielded to the indwelling Holy Spirit who imparts the life of Christ and who takes the things of Christ and shows them unto us.

Blessed Holy Spirit, give us a passion to know more and more of Him that filleth all in all. Amen.

252. OUR PEACE

For he is our peace, who hath made both one, and hath broken down the middle wall of partition between us.
EPHESIANS 2:14

"He is our Peace." Thank God, we have everything in Him. In the poor, old world, we have tribulations, trials, disappointments, sorrows of all kinds, but there never will be a time when we may not pillow our heads upon His shoulder and be at peace. Christ has reconciled both Jew and Gentile and the old wall of separation is broken down. He has reconciled men with God. Remember His words that last night with His disciples: "Peace I leave with you; my peace I give unto you. Let not your hearts be troubled, neither let them be afraid."

Blessed Lord Christ, we look to Thee with glad hearts and pray that the peace of God that passeth understanding may garrison our souls today. Amen.

---

253. ONE LORD

One Lord, one faith, one baptism.
EPHESIANS 4:5

The apostle is stating in this and the succeeding verses a great truth concerning the church. There is a seven-fold unity. One *body*—composed of believers. One *Spirit*—the Holy Spirit who dwells within every believer and unites them together in the common bond. One *hope*—the blessed hope of His coming. One *Lord*—the Lord over all. One *faith*—and that founded on the one Lord. One *baptism*—and that the baptism of the Holy Spirit. One *God and Father* of all—the object of our faith and in whose name all believers are baptized. We are not our own. We were bought with a great price. We are His subjects, under His rule and authority.

Lord Jesus, let us bow to Thee as the one Lord, and
with loyal hearts yield to Thy authority. Amen.

---

254. THE HEAD

But speaking the truth in love, may grow up into
him in all things, which is the head, even Christ.
EPHESIANS 4:15

We have already viewed Christ as the "Head over all things," but here we have Him as the Head of the body of believers—the church. There is inspiration in this thought—that we are to grow up into Him. How are we to do this? We have His life within us. The Head dominates the body and according to the need, the supply is furnished. The new nature demands a supply which cannot come from any other source than the Head. What a wonderful body the church would be, were it always mindful of its Head and responding to His desire for it!

Lord, help us to look unto Thee, Thou great
Head of the Church, and as members of
Thy body, grow into Thy likeness. Amen.

255. AN OFFERING

And walk in love, as Christ also hath loved us,
and hath given himself for us an offering.
EPHESIANS 5:2

Hear Him speaking that last night, "Greater love hath no man than this that a man lay down his life for his friends." What an offering for those disciples who deserted Him that very night! He became sin for us. He said, concerning the offering of His life, "I have power to lay it down and power to take it up." No man could take His life without His consent, who through the eternal Spirit offered Himself without spot to God.

Lord Jesus, we recognize Thy offering in our behalf.
Help us to walk in love as Thou hast also loved us, and
may our fellowship with Thee be sweet this day. Amen.

---

256. A SACRIFICE TO GOD

And walk in love, as Christ also hath loved us,
and hath given himself. . .a sacrifice to God.
EPHESIANS 5:2

God's holiness and righteousness demanded some way by which sin could be forgiven and removed, so that sinful men could have access to Him and live in fellowship with Him. There was only one way. Sin—violation of law—must be punished and the sinner must be justified from all things. The law of Moses could not do this. The offerings of the Old Testament could not do it. But God had a way. So "now once in the end of the age hath he appeared to put away sin by the sacrifice of Himself." "It is finished" were His words on the cross. Through His sacrifice our sins were washed away and rights and titles to Heaven granted us.

Lord, forbid that we should ever hesitate
to sacrifice all for Thee! Amen.

---

257. A SWEET-SMELLING SAVOUR

And walk in love, as Christ also hath loved us,
and hath given himself. . .for a sweetsmelling savour.
EPHESIANS 5:2

When Noah came out of the ark he took of every clean beast and of every clean fowl and offered a burnt offering unto the Lord. "And the Lord smelled a sweet savour." When Christ laid down His life on the cross what a perfume went up to God—the perfume from the sacrifice of His Son! Has the perfume of the cross yet reached you? It reached Heaven. Has the love of God, as manifested in the sacrifice of His Son, mastered you?

Our Father, forgive us that we have been so unmindful
of the wonders of Thy love. May its perfume pervade
our lives, and through us, the lives of others. Amen.

258. A SERVANT

But made himself of no reputation, and took upon him the form of a servant, and was made in the likeness of men.
PHILIPPIANS 2:7

Isaiah spoke concerning Him: "Behold, my Servant shall deal prudently. He shall be exalted and extolled very high." "His visage was marred more than any man." The meaning of the word "servant" is "a doer" or "a slave." He was God manifest in the flesh, but "He emptied himself," made Himself of "no reputation." Christ is the second Adam. He is the representative of perfect manhood. As a servant, He humbled Himself. From what lofty heights—Creator of all things down to a servant of men, step by step in service to the whipping post and the cross. What an example for us is He—the Servant!

Oh, Christ our Beloved, help us to follow in Thy footsteps and be in deed and in truth Thy chosen servants. Amen.

---

259. THE LORD JESUS CHRIST

To the saints and faithful brethren in Christ which are at Colosse: Grace be unto you, and peace, from God our Father and the Lord Jesus Christ.
COLOSSIANS 1:2

Master! Saviour! Anointed! Here, as in many other places in the epistles, we have a combination of names. "Grace and peace from God the Father and the Lord Jesus Christ." They are One. Mystery of mysteries! Hundreds of names and titles are given to Him, but after all, He has said, "I and my Father are One. He that hath seen Me hath seen the Father." When He descends from Heaven we will see Him in whom all of these titles are vested. Grace has its fountain in Him, and always in every emergency and under every condition and circumstance, His grace will be sufficient.

Gracious Lord Jesus Christ, manifest
Thy grace unto us today. Amen.

---

260. HIS DEAR SON

Who hath delivered us from the power of darkness, and
hath translated us into the kingdom of his dear Son.
COLOSSIANS 1:13

To "His dear Son" is here attributed the deliverance and translation of the believer from the power of Satan, the ruler of this dark world. Ignorant of Him, millions are dwelling today, controlled by the power of a Satanic nature, resisting His Word, and doomed to eternal darkness. There is but One who can deliver men. It is *His dear Son.* We are the possessors of this truth and have experienced it. How can we, how dare we, be indifferent to the blinded souls all around us when His dear Son is longing to have them respond to His call, "Come unto Me"?

Oh, Thou beloved Son, make us light-bearers
to darkened souls today. Amen.

261. THE IMAGE OF
THE INVISIBLE GOD

Who is the image of the invisible God,
the firstborn of every creature.
COLOSSIANS 1:15

It is difficult for us to refrain from loud acclamation as we view this expression concerning our Lord, the very "Image of the Invisible God"! We look at Him and we see God. We hear His voice and we hear God. We see Him holding the children in His arms, and we see God. We see Him in the home of friends, and we see God. We see Him feeding the multitudes, and we see God. There is but *one* God, and He is the One. "Great is the mystery!" Great is our expectation! Glory to God in the highest! We know Him. We love Him. We wait with longing hearts for Him.

Lord Jesus, in whom dwelleth all the fullness
of the Godhead bodily, we worship Thee!
We adore Thee! We look and long for Thee. Amen.

---

262. THE FIRST-BORN
OF EVERY CREATURE

Who is the image of the invisible God,
the firstborn of every creature.
COLOSSIANS 1:15

"The first-born of every creature," meaning "of every thing made." So many statements in the Scripture make plain the fact that God and Christ are One. He is the manifestation of God. He unites man and God. The invisible God has become visible to men, in Jesus Christ. He is the Sovereign Lord of creation by primogeniture; the Head of the natural creation and of the new creation, so that He is intimately allied to us. He is the first begotten from the dead. We could write a book about it, but a Book *has* been written.

Blessed Lord, our First-born, to whom we are united forever, help us to glorify Thee today. Amen.

263. CREATOR OF ALL THINGS

For by him were all things created.
COLOSSIANS 1:16

He is the Creator of *all* things—visible and invisible! Tarry a moment. Do not allow the magnitude of this revelation to escape you as your eyes are resting upon your loving Lord. Are we not prone to underestimate Him and undervalue His Work? See how Paul visualizes it in Ephesians 3:8–9: "Unto me, who am less than the least of all saints, is this grace given, that I should preach among the Gentiles the unsearchable riches of Christ. And to make all men see what is the fellowship of the mystery, which from the beginning of the world hath been hid in God, who created all things by Jesus Christ." Should we not take a place lower than Paul who counted himself the least of all saints?

Lord, help us. Keep ambition and pride from dominating us. Keep us at Thy feet in worship and praise. Amen.

264. THE HEAD OF THE BODY

And he is the head of the body, the church: who
is the beginning, the firstborn from the dead;
that in all things he might have the preeminence.
COLOSSIANS 1:18

The Word of God emphasizes this fact over and over again, and we need to have it emphasized so that we can be always viewing Him in the proper spirit. The church is His Body. We are members of that Body. We are One with Him. What is involved in this? We must recognize our relationship and think of Him always as our Head, and look to Him for wisdom and guidance. We must joyfully seek to walk in fellowship with Him, do His good pleasure, and in all things please Him.

Lord Jesus, Thou great Head of the Church, help us
to honor Thee this day by lip and life. Amen.

---

265. THE BEGINNING

Who is the beginning, the firstborn from the dead.
COLOSSIANS 1:18

He is the Beginning. Who is? The "First-born from the dead." By His resurrection, He inaugurated a new era, the beginning of a new life—eternal life. He is the "first-fruits of them that slept," the Prince of life. He solved the problem forever. He rose from the dead. He conquered death. His resurrection assures the resurrection of the bodies of all those who sleep in Him. The mystery is solved. There can be no end to this eternal life which we have through faith in Him, for it is His life. Let us stop and meditate today upon all that it means.

> *Thou blessed Lord, who art the beginning*
> *of that life in us that is insured forever,*
> *help us to tell the story to others. Amen.*

---

266. THE FIRST-BORN FROM THE DEAD

And he is. . .the firstborn from the dead; that in
all things he might have the preeminence.
COLOSSIANS 1:18

Here we have the origin of Christ's headship. "He is the first-fruits of them that sleep," or "have fallen asleep." He is the Originator of spiritual life, "The Beginning of the new creation of God." He died and was among the dead. Through death, He paid the penalty for sin and was raised for our justification "from *among* the dead." Others were translated or were raised but died again. He rose to die no more. This resurrection guarantees His headship and insures the resurrection of all believers. He has the preeminence in all things.

> *Our Lord Jesus, we glorify Thy name as the*
> *First-Born from the Dead and look forward*
> *to the day when we also shall be raised and, with*
> *glorified bodies, abide with Thee forever. Amen.*

267. HOPE OF GLORY

To whom God would make known what is the riches
of the glory of this mystery among the Gentiles;
which is Christ in you, the hope of glory.
COLOSSIANS 1:27

Here is a revelation not made known in other ages to the sons of men but now revealed by the Holy Spirit to the church. Paul is continually impressing the wonderful truth of God's will as the cause and work of salvation, and the wonderful privilege bestowed upon him of preaching it. This glory which is so wonderful is the garment with which all believers will be clothed when the Christ comes for us. How we should prize the possession of "Christ in us." Do we, and do we long that others might possess it also?

Lord, give us a hunger for others that they might
also be the rich possessors of the Hope of Glory. Amen.

---

268. CHRIST OUR LIFE

When Christ, who is our life, shall appear,
then shall ye also appear with him in glory.
COLOSSIANS 3:4

Hallelujah! What a promise is this: "When He shall appear!" He shall change these bodies of our abasement and fashion them like unto His own glorious body. Our life is in Him, "For me to live is Christ." He could not appear without us. He is preparing a place for us. He is coming for us. The anticipation of this is the great incentive of our life. These mortal bodies will be clothed like unto His glorious body. There can be no condition in life here which can rob us of the joy of this great truth. Let us breathe this atmosphere and look forward to that glorious day of our manifestation.

Our Lord, our Life, we will seek to honor Thee this day and pray that it may be a glad day. Amen.

---

269. ALL AND IN ALL

Where there is neither Greek nor Jew, circumcision nor uncircumcision, Barbarian, Scythian, bond nor free: but Christ is all, and in all.
COLOSSIANS 3:11

Christ is the Creator of all things. "Without Him was not anything made that was made." He is in all things. In Him we live and move and have our being. He is the beginning and the end of all things. He is the criterion by which all things must be measured. All power is in Him. All dominion, all authority is vested in Him. All distinctions are swept away. There is neither Jew nor Greek, old or young, rich or poor, learned or ignorant, bond or free. He unifies all by His indwelling Holy Spirit.

Lord, help us to recognize this blessed truth, enjoy it, abide in it and so glorify Thee this day. Amen.

270. THE LORD CHRIST

*Knowing that of the Lord ye shall receive the reward
of the inheritance: for ye serve the Lord Christ.*
COLOSSIANS 3:24

We are servants of the Lord Christ. We may never receive
what we think we should, or what we hope for, in this
world, but we are sure of a proper compensation when
God's books are opened, and He will render to every man
according to his deed. Earthly masters will disappoint
us; our Heavenly Master—never! No greater privilege
was ever accorded to men than that of serving the Lord
Christ. Let us seek to keep this in mind day by day. We
are heirs to a wonderful inheritance and our portion will
be assigned to us. What a joy to be a servant to such a
Master!

*Lord Christ, may our eyes be upon Thee as we take up
the tasks of the day and joyfully serve Thee. Amen.*

---

271. LORD OF PEACE

*Now the Lord of peace himself give you peace always
by all means. The Lord be with you all.*
2 THESSALONIANS 3:16

Our Lord is the Author of peace. He came to make peace
possible. "Peace I leave with you; My peace I give you." In
order to have this wonderful peace we must be yoked up
close to Himself. We live in a world of unrest and conflict.
The heart of humanity beats high with excitement. "No

peace for the wicked!" How we should pity them. They do not know Him. They can never know Him unless He is revealed to them. We are His spokesmen. Let us cheerfully make Him manifest today.

Lord of Peace, we pillow our heads upon Thy bosom. Thy peace passeth understanding. We thank Thee. Amen.

---

272. OUR HOPE

Paul, an apostle of Jesus Christ by the commandment of God our Saviour, and Lord Jesus Christ, which is our hope.
1 TIMOTHY 1:1

He is "our Hope." His promises assure us and fix our faith upon Him. He is the center of the life of a true believer. We could not think of the coming glory without eyes fixed upon Him. The incentive of a loyal life is to please Him. What could be more satisfying after a day of toil and burden-bearing than to remember how His Word was our comfort and His promises our peace? We look at the rising sun as it bathes the mountain peaks with its glory, and at the glittering stars at night and they foretell the coming of the glorious day when He will have us with Himself.

Lord, our Hope, our faith is fixed on Thee.
Help us to rest upon Thee this day. Amen.

273. CHRIST JESUS

Christ Jesus came into the world to
save sinners; of whom I am chief.
1 TIMOTHY 1:15

"The Anointed Saviour" came into the world to save sinners. Where did He come from? He came from the glory. Who was He? He was God, the Creator. "I came forth from the Father and am come into the world," He says in John 16:28. Sin separates man from God and separates God from man. Sin is opposition to God. Mankind is under the curse of sin and has no power to atone (make a covering) for its sin. God alone could meet the issue and solve the problem and He has. He came and bore man's sin on the cross and paid the penalty with His own blood.

We bow in Thy presence, Anointed Saviour,
and pour out our souls with gratitude to Thee.
Help us to live close to Thee today. Amen.

---

274. THE MEDIATOR

For there is one God, and one mediator
between God and men, the man Christ Jesus.
1 TIMOTHY 2:5

God is One and there is but one Mediator between God and man and that is a Man; but that Man—praise God—is the man Christ Jesus. He is the Mediator of the New Testament, for by means of death for the redemption of men He alone is qualified to act in man's behalf. He loved us. He died for us. Christ is God, but Christ is also the Head of humanity and He alone is capable of filling the position of Mediator. How wonderful He is, and He is all we need.

Blessed Mediator, our Sin-bearer, we open our hearts to Thee as we confess our sins and look with satisfaction upon the blood of Thy atonement. Amen.

275. THE MAN CHRIST JESUS

For there is one God, and one mediator between God and men, the man Christ Jesus.
1 TIMOTHY 2:5

We have considered Christ as Mediator and now we have the emphasis upon Christ, our Mediator, as the *Man* Christ Jesus. In these days when He is being demeaned by so many who are robbing Him of His Deity, we should rejoice in the privilege offered us of magnifying Him as both man and God. "Great is the mystery of Godliness—God manifest in the flesh." No picture in the Bible is so marvellously thrilling, so calculated to convince and convert, as that of God dying for men. Hold Him in your thoughts and see Him today—arms outstretched above a blood-stained body, saying, "Come unto Me. I will give you rest."

Oh, Thou crucified, risen God-Man, we adore Thee. Guide us today in our worship and work for Thee. Amen.

276. GOD MANIFEST IN THE FLESH

And without controversy great is the mystery of godliness:
God was manifest in the flesh, justified in the Spirit,
seen of angels, preached unto the Gentiles, believed
on in the world, received up into glory.
1 TIMOTHY 3:16

Here is a sermon of marvellous mystery. In a few words we have given to us the magnitude of the mission of Christ in leaving the glory and coming to this earth, clothed in the garments of flesh; accomplishing His Divine mission of redemption while in human form; leaving His witnesses to His crucifixion, resurrection, and ascension to His high and holy place in glory. We should stand with uncovered heads and with hearts beating in adoration, worship Him as the Holy Spirit of God emphasizes to us this great truth: He came, He died, He lives in us, and He lives in the glory, and we will dwell forever with Him.

Holy Spirit, help us to magnify
and glorify the God-Man. Amen.

---

277. BLESSED AND ONLY POTENTATE

Which in his times he shall shew, who is the blessed and
only Potentate, the King of kings, and Lord of lords.
1 TIMOTHY 6:15

This term is used but once in the Bible and means the "All Powerful One." Limitless power is His. It is to be manifested at His appearing who is King of kings and

Lord of lords. This will be the final event. Our Lord will reveal Himself and will bring with Him the crowns for the victors who have waged a good warfare and stand ready to receive the promised prize, which none can dispute His authority or right to bestow. Paul is so overcome with this vision that he breaks forth in notes of highest acclaim (read the sixteenth verse).

Oh, Thou Mighty One, we unite with Thy servant Paul and ascribe honor and power unto Thy name. Amen.

---

278. THE JUDGE OF QUICK AND DEAD

I charge thee therefore before God, and the Lord Jesus Christ, who shall judge the quick and the dead. . . . Preach the Word.

2 TIMOTHY 4:1–2

The Christian life is a solemnly serious life to live. It is a stewardship, and a day of accounting must come. We must *all* appear before Him to give an account for the deeds done in the body. There is no escape from our responsibility for obedience to the command, "Preach (tell) the Word (of God); be instant in season and out of season." How solemn! Every man's work will be tried by fire of what sort it is. Gold, silver, precious stones; wood, hay, stubble! It is for us to decide. No one can change the record—neither God nor man. Are you ready?

Lord Jesus, we look for Thy coming. Help us to do our best today to make Thy will and Thy way known. Amen.

279. THE RIGHTEOUS JUDGE

Henceforth there is laid up for me a crown of righteousness, which the Lord, the righteous judge, shall give me at that day.

2 TIMOTHY 4:8

In the judgment spoken of here there is a promised reward which Paul speaks of as coming to himself and to all those who love the truth concerning the coming of the Lord. They are to be crowned and the Lord will Himself put the crown upon the head of those who are true to His promises and look for Him—a "crown of righteousness." There are many crowns awaiting the saints. Salvation is a *gift*, but crowns are for those whose lives have been lived in obedience to the Word of God. His shed blood should be the appeal to us to be willing to lay down our lives for Him.

Lord Jesus, give us an increasing desire to see Thee and be with Thee. Help us to complete the Body and thus hasten Thy coming. Amen.

---

280. THE GREAT GOD

Looking for that blessed hope, and the glorious appearing of the great God and our Saviour Jesus Christ.

TITUS 2:13

For whom are we looking? Everywhere it is stated in the Scripture that we are to look for our Lord—for Jesus Christ who died. "This same Jesus shall so come as ye have seen Him go." He will come with His glorified body; with the hands that were pierced; with the wounded side from which the life-blood was poured out; with the scarred brow where the thorns left their marks. The same voice that said, "Behold my hands and my feet. It is I, be not afraid," will welcome us when we meet Him in the air.

Lord Jesus, we wait with expectant hearts,
and our voices are tuned for the Hallelujah
Chorus as we say, "Come." Amen.

281. GOD OUR SAVIOUR

But after that the kindness and love of
God our Saviour toward man appeared.
Titus 3:4

This is not the first time that the title "God our Saviour" has been used. We find it in 1 Timothy 1:1, where the reference, no doubt, is to the call of Paul as recorded in Acts 13:2. Here it refers to God as our Saviour. Jesus said, "I and my Father are one," and He is our Saviour. When we sing "Saviour, More Than Life to Me," we recognize the almighty power and authority of God our Saviour. Let us look up to Him today. By our God-given right we have been regenerated and renewed by the Holy Spirit and should exercise our rights as His children.

Let us open wide the door of our hearts to Thee, our God
and Saviour, and give Thee the right of way today. Amen.

282. HEIR OF ALL THINGS

Hath in these last days spoken unto us by his Son,
whom he hath appointed heir of all things,
by whom also he made the worlds.

HEBREWS 1:2

How logical the Bible is. To our Lord is ascribed glory because He is the Creator of all things. He made the worlds. He says, "All things that the Father hath are Mine." Unlimited power is His. Unlimited possessions are His. We are also His. Praise God, what a revelation we have of Him! He purchased us with His own precious blood. We are dear to Him as the apple of His eye. He will never leave us nor forsake us. We belong to the "Heir of all things." Our needs will be supplied, then, for we are heirs of God and joint-heirs with Jesus Christ. Let us keep our heads erect and our eyes turned heavenward.

Thou blessed "Heir of all things," take us under
Thy wings today and may we be gloriously
happy in fellowship with Thee. Amen.

---

283. THE BRIGHTNESS OF HIS GLORY

Who being the brightness of his glory.
HEBREWS 1:3

Do you want to visualize the glory of God? Then gaze upon Jesus Christ. When we see Him, we see God, for He is God. Oh, the marvel of the God-head! How wonderful it is! How fascinating is this Bible of ours in which we have such a revelation of God as manifest in the flesh! Moses prayed to God, "I beseech Thee, shew me Thy glory," and the answer was, "I will make all My goodness pass before thee." With your Bible in hand, meditate upon this revelation of Jesus Christ and rejoice in Him as your own Lord.

Father, let the rays of sunshine from the person
of Christ shine in our hearts today. Amen.

---

284. THE EXPRESS IMAGE OF HIS PERSON

Who being the brightness of his glory,
and the express image of his person.
HEBREWS 1:3

"No man hath seen God at any time. The only begotten Son, who is in the bosom of the Father, He hath declared Him." We have seen the Father for we have seen the Son. We have seen Him, a man among men, eating, drinking, living, working with them. When a seal is stamped upon a piece of paper, we have its exact image. When we see Jesus we see the God-Man—a *perfect* representation of God, and we see the *only* God we will ever see. Hold that truth and meditate upon it for awhile, and let the Holy Spirit magnify Christ to you. Thank God, we have seen Him, we know Him, we love Him, we are one with Him.

Lord, let us bask in the sunshine of Thy love
today and mould and fashion us more and
more in conformity to Thy image. Amen.

285. THE UPHOLDER OF ALL THINGS

Who being the brightness of his glory, and the
express image of his person, and upholding
all things by the word of his power.
HEBREWS 1:3

God is Light. Jesus is the radiance of that light. God is the Sun and Jesus is the Sunbeam. The sun and sunshine are co-existent. We see the *sunbeam*, not the sun itself, but the *rays* of the sun. If you break a sun-beam through a prism, you have all the colors. When Jesus was broken on the cross, all of the richness of the glory of God was manifested. He is the express image of the person of God. He is the Upholder of all things. He created all things. He purged all sin. In the hollow of His hand are all things. You can trust all to Him.

Lord Jesus, we thank Thee for Thy finished
work. We rest in Thee. Keep us trustful
and faithful until Thy coming. Amen.

---

286. THE SIN PURGER

Who. . .when he had by himself purged our sins,
sat down on the right hand of the Majesty on high.
HEBREWS 1:3

How lightly we think of sin. It is so common that we fail to view it in God's light. "Coming short of the glory of God" is sin. Sin has never changed because human nature has never changed. Every child born into this world is born with the Adam and Eve nature. There is no exception. One sin makes a sinner and shuts the door to Heaven. Christ came as the Sin-purger and opened the door to Heaven. We need only to tell our fellowmen the story and point them to the open door. "I am the Door," He says. "By *Me*, if *any* man enter in he shall be saved." God help us to tell hungry-hearted men the story.

Oh, Thou Sin-purger, we give unto Thee
all the praise and ask for tender hearts in
telling the story to sinful men. Amen.

---

287. GOD

But unto the Son he saith, Thy throne,
O God, is for ever and ever.
HEBREWS 1:8

Here we have the Alpine height in titles for our Lord, "Thy throne, O *God*"! All other names are inferior to this. When He was born in a manger, God was there. When He worked at the carpenter's trade, God was there at work. When He associated with the fishermen, it was God who was their companion. When He spoke, God spoke. When He died on the cross, it was God Himself who poured out His life. When He comes "with a shout," it will be the voice of God that calls us to be with Him forever. It is God the Son who holds the sceptre and rules the worlds, and we will rule and reign with Him.

Oh, God our Saviour and Coming King, hasten Thy
coming, and help us to help Thee hasten that day,
for Thine own name's sake. Amen.

288. THE CAPTAIN
OF OUR SALVATION

For it became him. . .to make the captain
of their salvation perfect through sufferings.
HEBREWS 2:10

We cannot but bow our heads as we read this verse
and meditate upon the Captain of our salvation and
His perfection. He was God and He was Man, we have
learned. As Man He must be manifest in the life. He is
the Son of God, the Captain (or "Author") of salvation.
We are the *sons* of God. The mode and method of
perfection is manifested by our Leader. He was tempted;
so are we. He suffered; so must we. He was persecuted;
so must we be. He paid the price; so must we. The climax
for Him and for us is glory.

Let us bow our heads and hearts to our Leader
today and obey His orders. He will be with
us in every trial and suffering. Amen.

---

289. THE SEED OF ABRAHAM

For verily he took not on him the nature of angels;
but he took on him the seed of Abraham.
HEBREWS 2:16

This suggestive title surely draws a picture well worthy
our consideration. Why did He not take on Himself the
nature of angels? Do not the fallen angels need help? Are
they inferior to men? Will they evolve into good angels?

No, but those angels who fell, did so in full consciousness of all that it meant. He came to fallen man and took upon Himself the "seed of Abraham" because He longed to lift us to heights above those ever known to angels.

Our Lord, the wonder of Thy work for us astonishes us. Keep us, we pray Thee, from being selfish. Help us to tell the story of Thy love to our fellowmen. Amen.

290. THE APOSTLE

Consider the Apostle and High Priest of our profession, Christ Jesus.
HEBREWS 3:1

Jesus was an Apostle (or "Sent One"). He was sent with the Gospel (Good News). God sent prophets and angels to bear His messages to men. He sent Moses, the mighty man of God. But now we are looking at the Apostle from Heaven's court itself. He came to bring the most wonderful message ever intended for mortal ears: "God so loved the world!" Why did He so love it, and how was that love manifested? This Apostle did His work and has appointed us, who are believers, to carry it on to fallen men. This Apostle was faithful. Are we? We are His authorized representatives.

Help us to be Thy "sent ones" today, bearing the joyful message of salvation to those who know it not. Amen.

291. THE HIGH PRIEST

Consider the. . .High Priest of
our profession, Christ Jesus.
HEBREWS 3:1

We are called to consider Jesus Christ as High Priest. We are called "holy brethren." We cannot be called upon too often to consider Him as our High Priest seeing that "he ever liveth to make intercession for us." Could we but make it our life habit to, every morning, spend a few moments in contemplation of Him as *our* High Priest, and take up life's duties with that picture before us, seeing Him clothed in the garments of the High Priest, in the Holy of Holies, we would be better believers.

May our eyes be upon Thee today,
Thou great High Priest. Amen.

---

292. THE BUILDER

For this man was counted worthy of more glory
than Moses, inasmuch as he who hath builded
the house hath more honour than the house.
HEBREWS 3:3

Christ is here set forth as "the Builder" or "Establisher" of the house. He is the Apostle. He is the High Priest. The foundation of the house is laid in Him. "Ye are God's building," Paul says in 1 Corinthians 3:9. We are temples of the Holy Spirit now. Christ dwells within us. We are to be built up into a holy temple from which will go forth the voices of millions of the redeemed as they sing the Hallelujah Chorus. Let Christ have His way in fitting us for our appointed places in the Temple of God, for He is the Master Builder and we are to share with Him in the coming day.

Grant unto us, Lord, submission to Thy
Holy will in all things this day. Amen.

---

293. THE GREAT HIGH PRIEST

Seeing then that we have a great high priest,
that is passed into the heavens, Jesus the Son
of God, let us hold fast our profession.
HEBREWS 4:14

Jesus, the Son of God, is our great High Priest. Where is He? In the glory, at the right hand of the glory of God. What is He there for? To represent us. He carried the blood offering with Him and presented it in the Holy of Holies. He has seated Himself. He is our representative. We can come with boldness to the throne of grace, and will find grace for every need. He is the Son of God with power. Let us hold fast our confession. He loves us. He took our place on the cross. He settled every claim against us. Satan may condemn us, but our great High Priest holds forth His pierced hands and that is enough.

Lord Jesus, while Thou art representing us in the
glory yonder, help us to represent Thee here. Amen.

294. A PRIEST FOREVER

Thou art a priest for ever after the order of Melchisedec.
HEBREWS 5:6

He is our High Priest, our Great High Priest, and He is also a *Priest forever* after the similitude of Melchisedec (Genesis 14:18–20), that strange character who typified our Lord. Will Christ be our representative throughout eternity? Yes—and *we* will be *His* representatives throughout eternity. For our new life is eternal. Our habitation will be eternal. How it warms our hearts to think of that word "forever" in connection with our relation to Christ! He is our eternal High Priest and we are to be kings and priests in association with Him (Revelation 1:6). We are poor, undone, hell-deserving sinners, but through Him, we are lifted to eternal heights.

*Lord, Thou great High Priest, help us
to honor Thee by lip and life. Amen.*

---

295. AUTHOR OF ETERNAL SALVATION

*And being made perfect, he became the author
of eternal salvation unto all them that obey him.*
HEBREWS 5:9

Christ was perfected through suffering. He was obedient unto death, even the death of the cross, and through the hard, cruel, sacrificial journey, which He made to the cross—suffering beyond the power of thought to comprehend—He perfected a way by which men could be saved. When He bore our sin on the cross, the unchanging law of God was in operation, and He suffered separation from God. There was but one way by which sinful men could be made righteous, and that was by the Saviour's taking our place, which He did, and now His obedient followers share with Him the glory.

In every time of testing, sorrow, or suffering,
may we look to Thee, our eternal salvation,
and find the promised comfort and help. Amen.

---

296. THE FORERUNNER

Whither the forerunner is for us entered, even Jesus.
HEBREWS 6:20

"Our hope is fixed on nothing less than Jesus' blood and righteousness." Our hope is an anchor which entereth into that which is beyond the veil, and our Forerunner has entered beyond the veil into the Holy of Holies. Our hope is anchored in Him. How safe it is! How satisfying it is! We are a part of Him. We can never be separated from Him because He lives in us and we shall live and be with Him forever. Let our souls go out in unbounded thanksgiving.

Lord Jesus, our great Forerunner, we rejoice in
Thee today. Thou art in the glory. We are looking
forward to being with Thee and like Thee.
Come quickly and receive us unto Thyself. Amen.

297. KING OF RIGHTEOUSNESS

First being by interpretation King of righteousness.
HEBREWS 7:2

The picture is taken from the story of Melchisedec, the strange king to whom Abram paid tithes (Genesis 14). Christ is King of righteousness, for He is the King of kings. He is *the* Righteous One and the *only* Righteous One. We have no righteousness. All of our righteousness is as filthy rags, but "Christ is the end of the law for righteousness to everyone that believeth." We believe in Him, and it is counted unto us for righteousness. His righteousness is put to our account and we are associated with the Righteous King forever. Hallelujah!

Lord, we confess our unworthiness, but we
rejoice in Thy finished work and in the
gift of Thy righteousness to us. Amen.

---

298. KING OF PEACE

After that also King of Salem, which is, King of peace.
HEBREWS 7:2

Righteousness is the basis of peace. There is no peace for the wicked. "He is our peace, who hath made both one, and hath broken down the middle wall of partition between Jew and Gentile, and hath made of twain one new man, so making peace." Remember what the King of Peace said, "Peace I leave with you; my peace I give unto you. Let not your heart be troubled, neither let it be afraid." He dwells in us and we dwell in Him. He came and preached peace. He went to the cross and made peace possible. "Great peace have they which love Thy law."

Oh, Thou King of Peace, may Thy peace which passeth all understanding, garrison our souls this day. Amen.

---

299. THE SURETY

By so much was Jesus made a surety of a better testament.
HEBREWS 7:22

Sometimes we lack assurance. We tremble, perhaps, and lack confidence in the finished work which our Christ has wrought for us. But we have here the statement that Christ has become our Surety, or Security. We are made confident by the fact that He has placed Himself as our Bondsman, our Security. We can draw our drafts upon the Bank of Heaven and He has pledged Himself as our Security. "Whatsoever ye shall ask in My name, that will I do." Why have we so little faith in His pledged Word? Giving doth not impoverish Him, nor withholding enrich Him.

Let us honor Him by asking today, in His precious Name, large things for His glory. Amen.

300. OUR INTERCESSOR

*Wherefore he is able also to save them to the
uttermost that come unto God by him, seeing
he ever liveth to make intercession for them.*
HEBREWS 7:25

He saves to the fullest extent for He ever liveth and He ever represents us and meets all the charges against us. "And He saw that there was no man, and wondered that there was no intercessor. Therefore His arm brought salvation unto Him; and His righteousness, it sustained Him" (Isaiah 59:16). The Holy Spirit also makes intercession for us with "groanings which cannot be uttered." Satan may bring charges against us, and sometimes they may be well founded, but He is there. He bore our sins, carried our sorrows, meets every accusation. What a wonderful Saviour and Intercessor!

*Our Lord, we draw near in full assurance of faith. Thou
wilt never leave us nor forsake us. We glorify Thy name
now and will ever throughout eternity. Amen.*

---

301. SEPARATE FROM SINNERS

*For such an high priest became us,
who is. . .separate from sinners.*
HEBREWS 7:26

We use this as a title (or attribute) of our Lord because preachers and teachers are drifting so far away from the belief in the Virgin Birth of Our Lord, denying that He was God manifest in the flesh and lining up with the

Unitarian belief. But remember the sin question could only be settled by a *sinless* Man—a *spotless* Lamb. Such was He who *knew* no sin though He *became* sin for us, that we might become the righteousness of God in Him. But, though He was separate from sinners, He did not avoid them as we are wont to do. No one ever loved them as He did—the Holy One. We must not miss this suggestion if we are to be like Him, loving sinners and following His example.

Lord Jesus, give us a REAL love for lost souls
and a passion for their salvation. Amen.

---

302. HIGHER THAN THE HEAVENS

For such an high priest became us,
who is. . .higher than the heavens.
HEBREWS 7:26

This wonderful High Priest, the spotless Lamb of God, when He had finished His priestly sin-offering, sat down at the right hand of God. Yet we can see Him, the unchangeable Christ, with wounded hands and feet bearing testimony to His individuality and unchanging personality. Some day from the dizzy heights He will descend with a shout. His voice will ring out in glad expectancy. He is coming for you and for me. Wonder of wonders! Our faith in His finished work has sealed us forever to Himself.

Lord, Thou exalted One, we give Thee all praise and
wait with glad hearts for Thy coming. Amen.

303. THE MINISTER
OF THE SANCTUARY

A minister of the sanctuary, and of the true tabernacle,
which the Lord pitched, and not man.

HEBREWS 8:2

We are carried back to the picture of the Tabernacle and of the Temple where God's High Priest officiated. He represented God in all of the ceremonies of the Holy Assembly. Here we have the promised Messiah, the Lord Jesus Christ, in the capacity of the Minister (or servant) of the Sanctuary. He is the King, but He is still a Servant of men, serving in our behalf, loving us, ministering to us. Dwelling in our heart by the Holy Spirit, He performs every needed function in the cleansing and preparing of His people for their access to God.

We thank Thee, Lord Jesus, for Thy
marvellous ministry in our behalf.

---

304. MEDIATOR OF
A BETTER COVENANT

But now. . .he is the mediator of a better covenant.

HEBREWS 8:6

We have viewed our Lord as "the Minister of the Sanctuary," and He is now termed the "Mediator of a Better Covenant." Aaron was the high priest of the sanctuary of the old covenant, but now Christ in Heaven is the Mediator of a Heavenly covenant—God's agreement to confer blessings upon men. He promises to put His laws into their minds and write them on their hearts and says, "I will be their God and they shall be My people; their sins and iniquities will I remember no more." Let us remember, then, that we are His sanctuary, His temple, and He will perfect His work in and through us. Give way to His will and let our temples be holy unto the Lord.

Help us, Thou great Mediator, to surrender all to Thee. Cleanse us, keep us cleansed that we may offer acceptable worship unto Thee. Amen.

---

305. THE TESTATOR

For where a testament is, there must also of necessity be the death of the testator.
HEBREWS 9:16

A testator is a man who makes and leaves a will, or testament, at death. Christ has left a testament and a will. He died for us. He shed His blood as a free-will offering in our behalf. Under the law we were condemned to death. "The soul that sinneth, it shall die." "Death passed upon all men in that all have sinned." The sin question is settled forever for us who believe in Jesus Christ, our Testator. He ever lives. He represents us in the presence of the Father.

Lord, we lift our hearts to Thee and rejoice in the finished work and testimony of our Testator. Amen.

306. HE THAT SHALL COME

For yet a little while, and he that shall
come will come, and will not tarry.
HEBREWS 10:37

The Christian life is built not only on the present but on the unseen future. Our life is a life of faith, a faith tried and tested and proven; fixed upon the unerring, unbreakable Word of God. God has never broken a promise and He never can. We can bank with unfailing confidence upon His Written and Living Word. Nothing pleases our Lord more than implicit faith in His Word and work. Nothing gives us such rest and joy as does this child-like faith. We must not be moved by the theories or doubts of men. When in doubt, read Hebrews eleven.

Lord, we are looking for Thy coming in
the clouds of glory. Come quickly! Amen.

---

307. A REWARDER

But without faith it is impossible to please him: for he
that cometh to God must believe that he is, and that
he is a rewarder of them that diligently seek him.
HEBREWS 11:6

We come to God only through Jesus Christ: "No man cometh unto the Father but by Me." And our Lord Jesus Christ is the Judge (John 5:22). "For the Father judgeth no man, but hath committed all judgment unto the Son." He pronounces the sentence. He gives the reward

(Revelation 22:12). "And, behold, I come quickly and my reward is with me." What we do we must do in His name and for His Glory (Colossians 3:24): "Knowing that of the Lord ye shall receive the reward of the inheritance: for ye serve the Lord Christ." We must live for Him and be willing to die for Him. Our reward awaits us.

Lord, we commit ourselves to Thee.
Use us this day for Thy glory. Amen.

308. THE FINISHER OF FAITH

Looking unto Jesus the. . .finisher of our faith.
HEBREWS 12:2

He is the Captain and leads His hosts with the Sword of the Spirit in His hand. And He is the Finisher (Completer) of our faith. Our Lord set us the example of faith and He will perfect it in us. We see Jesus who for the joy that was set before Him endured the cross, despised the shame and is now set down at the right hand of God. He *finished* His work of faith, and by grace He will finish it in our experience. There will be trials, there will be severe testings, but we are to "count it all joy." He did, and day by day and step by step, He leads us on. The best is always before us, though the last link may be the cross—but then, "Face to face with Him"!

Lord, hold us fast by the power of faith
until we finish our course. Amen.

309. THE AUTHOR OF FAITH

Looking unto Jesus the author. . .of our faith.
HEBREWS 12:2

The Author (Leader) of our faith is Jesus. Look to Him, for the inspiration to faith is found in Him. He is the prophesied and promised "Seed of the woman," bruised by Satan. He paid the penalty and then robbed the grave of its power, rose in the majesty of His glorified body, and will come some day to bruise the serpent's head, master and imprison him. He inspires us by His sacrificial death and by His precious promises. His message is "Follow me. I will never leave thee nor forsake thee." And our response to Him should be, "Lead on; we will follow Thee even unto death."

Oh, Thou great Author of our Faith, keep our
eyes on Thee and with unwavering faith
may we follow Thee to the end. Amen.

---

310. MEDIATOR OF
THE NEW COVENANT

And to Jesus the mediator of the new covenant,
and to the blood of sprinkling, that speaketh
better things than that of Abel.
HEBREWS 12:24

The Christian life is a strange life, a journey through wilderness experiences, but we always have something better before us. The door posts are sprinkled with blood. We are safe. Old things have passed away. The blood of Jesus Christ, God's Son, cleanseth us from *all* sin. The blood speaks of His sacrificial, finished work. Let our eyes rest upon the cross. Let us see the blood. Let us rest under it. Let it separate us from a sinful world and make of us witnesses to its cleansing power, and let us magnify its efficacy to a sin-sick world.

Lord, give us the needed grace to witness today and every day to the efficacy of the atoning blood of the New Covenant. Amen.

---

311. MY HELPER

So that we may boldly say, The Lord is my helper.
HEBREWS 13:6

What a difference there is in believers! How timid some are. Is it because they do not know the promises? "The fear of man bringeth a snare; but whoso trusteth the Lord shall be safe." "The angel of the Lord encampeth round about them that fear him and delivereth them." Courage of conviction is the crying need of the Christian today— conviction based on God's Holy Word and God's call to service. He hath said, "I will never leave thee nor forsake thee." Faith takes hold upon this promise and allows nothing to move it.

Lord Jesus, our Helper, help us to lean hard upon Thy gracious promises and have a joyful life today. Amen.

312. JESUS CHRIST THE SAME

Jesus Christ the same yesterday,
and to day, and for ever.
HEBREWS 13:8

"The Same!" How we love this verse. The world is a sinful, restless world. Uncertainty is written everywhere in human life, but the Living Word and the Written Word are unchangeable. What was He before He was born of the Virgin Mary? He was God. What was He when He lived and labored among men? He was God. What was He when He hung on the Cross? He was God. What is He today? Still God, with the same pierced hands and feet, the same scarred side, the same loving heart—for having loved His own, He loves them still and will love them throughout eternity. Nothing in human thought or language is more wonderful.

Lord Jesus Christ, Thou art the same. Help us to
sense it and intensify our love for Thee and
may it also be always "the same." Amen.

313. THE GREAT SHEPHERD OF THE SHEEP

Our Lord Jesus, that great shepherd of the sheep.
HEBREWS 13:20

In the sixth chapter of Mark we have a touching picture of our Lord Jesus. He had been apart with His disciples in a desert place, and "when He saw much people He was moved with compassion toward them, because they were as sheep not having a shepherd, and He began to teach them many things." He was the promised Shepherd. He is here pictured as the Great Shepherd, raised from the dead, sanctified by the blood of the everlasting covenant, which is able to make us "perfect in every good work to do His will" (verse 21). How? By working in us and through us that which pleases Himself.

Lord, we are Thy sheep. Take us, mould us,
and make of us that which shall please Thee,
and we will give Thee all the glory. Amen.

314. THAT WORTHY NAME

Do not they blaspheme that worthy
name by the which ye are called?
JAMES 2:7

James is dealing here with the theme of prayer. He urges the saints not to have the faith with respect to persons, and gives them a needed lesson on partiality in our attitude toward men because of their wealth or position. The emphasis is on "The Worthy Name." That Name is sacred, "for there is none other Name. . .whereby we must be saved." "God has given Him a Name which is above every name; that at the Name Jesus every knee should bow," though for some who are compelled to bow, it will be too late. In that Name we approach our Father; in that Name we have our title to the glory land.

*Lord Jesus, we come in Thy Worthy Name and
ask for forgiveness for our sins of neglect and
ask for Thy power for service this day. Amen.*

---

315. A LAMB WITHOUT BLEMISH OR SPOT

*But with the precious blood of Christ, as of
a lamb without blemish and without spot.*
1 PETER 1:19

Our familiarity with Scriptural terms often causes us
to minimize their meaning. Here we have two words
so marvellously wonderful that we are hesitant in our
effort to make any comment—"Blood" and "Lamb."
How precious the Blood! Millions and millions of drops
were poured out through the ages from Abel to Christ
and every one of them said: "The Lamb is not yet. But
He will come. We are the testimony of His coming."
And finally the Spotless, Pure Lamb of God finished the
work of redemption. Is He precious to us? So precious
that we would be willing to die in His behalf? If so, let
us say to Him,

*Oh, Lamb of God, my Saviour, purchased by Thy
precious blood, I surrender all to Thee now. Amen.*

316. A CHIEF CORNER STONE

Behold, I lay in Sion a chief corner stone. . .and he
that believeth on him shall not be confounded.

1 PETER 2:6

Every structure must have a foundation and those of
special honor must have a corner-stone. Christ is the
Chief Corner Stone of the most wonderful temple ever
conceived. This temple is built of human lives—blood-
washed saints of the Living God. It is the dwelling place
of God the Father, God the Son, and God the Holy
Spirit. Over the doors are inscribed the words, "Holiness
unto the Lord." From the dome the chimes ring out the
call, "Exalt the Lord our God and worship at His feet."

Oh, Lord, may we be the mouth-pieces to
spread the invitation to others to come
to the temple for worship. Amen.

---

317. A LIVING STONE

To whom coming, as unto a living stone, disallowed
indeed of men, but chosen of God, and precious.

1 PETER 2:4

Words are inadequate to describe the mysteries of
Heaven. It is not composed of an inert mass like the
stones of earth, but of *living, life-imparting* stones. He
is living. He will always be living. He lives in the lives of
the redeemed. He is the chosen of God. He is the Stone
cut out of the mountain which is to crush the nations.

He is the One in whom and through whom we have everlasting life. He lives and will live through eternity and we will live in and with Him. Hallelujah!

Dear Lord, our Rock, our Foundation Stone,
we rest in the security of Thy eternal life.
Manifest that life through us today. Amen.

---

318. AN ELECT STONE

Behold, I lay in Sion a chief corner stone, elect. . .
1 PETER 2:6

The Elect Stone (the "Chosen of God") is the Chief Corner Stone of the Temple of God, which is composed of believers who were chosen before the foundation of the world. Nothing ever occurs by chance with God. He saw this Temple before He created the universe. We were chosen in Him, our Lord, and He was chosen in the Council Chamber of Heaven to become the Elect Stone—the One who should be the Head of the Corner. His plans are all working out for the culminating scene when the gathering shall take place at His coming.

When the time comes, Lord Jesus, may we be among
those who will bring our sheaves with us. Amen.

319. A PRECIOUS STONE

Behold, I lay in Sion a chief corner stone. . .precious.
1 PETER 2:6

How precious He is! The more we know about Him the more wonderful He becomes, and the more intimately we know Him the more precious He is. "To whom coming as unto a living stone, disallowed indeed of men, but chosen of God and *precious*." Not precious to the world, for the world has no place, no use for Him; but "unto you who believe He is precious." He is the Creator. He holds the world in the hollow of His hand as a dry leaf and could crush it. But He so loved you and me that He laid aside His royal robe, arrayed Himself in human flesh, and then poured out His precious blood for us. Should He not be precious to us?

Lord, we desire in our hearts to hold Thee
PRECIOUS. Holy Spirit, help us. Amen.

---

320. A STONE OF STUMBLING

The stone which the builders disallowed. . .
is made. . .a stone of stumbling.
1 PETER 2:7–8

A Corner Stone upon which the whole world was built, upon which the church is built, and a "Stone of Stumbling"! How can that be? To those who willfully reject Him, as did the Jewish nation, and stumble into the abyss, there is weeping and wailing and gnashing of teeth. To those who pride themselves upon their education, wealth or position, and refuse to bow at His feet, He is a Stone of Stumbling. How subtle is Satan! How hard is the human heart! How our hearts ache for those who know Him not.

Our Lord, Thou art precious to us. Help us to remove the stumbling blocks by living out a life that shall win some souls to Thee. Amen.

321. A ROCK OF OFFENSE

The stone which the builders disallowed. . . is made. . .a rock of offence.
1 PETER 2:7–8

The Jewish nation is an illustration of our theme. Every possible effort was made by Christ to win His own people to Himself. But they would not have Him. What a blow has fallen upon them! Driven from pillar to post, peeled, robbed, persecuted, killed, their desire has been granted. "Let his blood be upon us and upon our children." How will it be in the future? See Revelation 6:15–16. How can it be that our loving, crucified Lord should become to so many a "Rock of Offense" instead of the "Chief Corner Stone"?

Our Lord, keep our feet on the Rock and our hearts loving Thee. Amen.

322. THE BISHOP OF SOULS

For ye were as sheep going astray; but are now returned
unto the Shepherd and Bishop of your souls.
1 PETER 2:25

The elders of the early church were "overseers"—called to care for the flock as under-shepherds. Here Christ is set before us as the One who directs the under-shepherds. He is *The Bishop*. He is the imparter of life which is eternal, which He purchased for us by His own sacrifice. His eye is upon us. He is the One whose heart goes out in love to the lost, straying sheep and who never fails in His own good way and time to bring them back to the fold (the true church). God help those who selfishly seek and faithlessly serve as under-shepherds. "Seekest thou great things for thyself? Seek them not."

Lord, help us to recognize Thee as our Bishop and be
subject to Thy guidance. Hold us. Keep us. Feed us. Amen.

---

323. THE JUST

For Christ also hath once suffered
for sins, the just for the unjust.
1 PETER 3:18

How strong is the contrast here—the *Just* for the *unjust*! Why this sacrifice? That He might bring us to God, making it possible for us to have access through the rent veil to the Holy of Holies. He was the *Just*, the *Sinless One*. "He became obedient unto death" bearing our sins that He might "bring us to God." Sin demands punishment. Jesus kept the law and took our place who were violators of law, setting us free from the penalty and according to us the rights and titles of "just ones." Think of the Cross, the agony, the pain, the shameful death—*all* for you and me!

Oh, Thou Just One, Thou who hast paid the penalty and the price for our sins, help us to bear Thee in our hearts today. Amen.

---

324. THE CHIEF SHEPHERD

And when the chief Shepherd shall appear, ye shall receive a crown of glory that fadeth not away.
1 PETER 5:4

Christ as our Shepherd has already been considered as the "Door of the Sheep," "The Good Shepherd," "The One Shepherd," "The Great Shepherd," and now we have the climax in "The Chief Shepherd." In Him is vested all authority and power. He will give the rewards to the faithful. His glory is to be shared by us. Our faithfulness to Him here is to be rewarded there. We visualize Him with shepherd staff leading, guiding, directing His sheep, and enfolding them in safety. But there is the glad day which is to come when He will crown His loyal ones. Is there anything more to be desired than the privilege accorded us of making Him now the chiefest of ten thousand in our hearts?

Lord, be Thou to us today the
Altogether Lovely One. Amen.

325. THE DAY STAR

We have also a more sure word of prophecy;
whereunto ye do well that ye take heed. . .
until. . .the day star arise in your hearts.
2 PETER 1:19

In the Gospel of John, we read: "In Him was life and the life was the Light of men." We have the sure Word of God. It is a lamp to our feet and a light unto our path. Our hearts are darkened by the evil nature within us, but when Jesus comes into our hearts He illumines the Word of God and shines with all the effulgence of His glory. Perpetual day is for those who walk in His light. Every day is a good day and the eternal glory awaits us.

Blessed Lord, our Light, shine in our hearts and
lives this day and may we reflect Thy glory. Amen.

326. LORD AND SAVIOUR JESUS CHRIST

But grow in grace, and in the knowledge
of our Lord and Saviour Jesus Christ.
2 PETER 3:18

"Grow in grace!" Thank God, it is possible and it is our bounden duty so to do. "And in the knowledge of—!"

Here we pause and face a most remarkable exhortation. The vastness of the suggestion of growing in the "knowledge of the Lord, the Saviour, Jesus, and Christ" sets before us a task which will last throughout eternity. Growing into Him—this marvellous One whom we do not know, thank God—is a part of eternal life. How shall we obey this command? Study His Word. It is the Lamp and Light. Search this Word. It is a mine of treasures. Submit to the commandments of the Word. Then will we be wise indeed.

Our Lord and Saviour, Jesus Christ, bowing in Thy glorious presence, we submit to Thee. Help us to know and love Thee more and more as the days go by. Amen.

327. THE WORD OF LIFE

That which. . .our hands have handled, of the Word of life.
1 JOHN 1:1

John 1:1–2 says: "In the beginning was the Word, and the Word was with God and the Word was God; the same was in the beginning with God," and this truth bewilders us; but here we have John saying concerning Him who was God that he had looked upon Him and handled Him. He, Himself, said to doubting Thomas, "Handle Me and see. A spirit hath not flesh and bones as ye see Me have." He is the Life-giving Word. The need of a lost world is to know Him. The business of believers is to tell the wonderful story. Paint the picture. Live the life. Sow the seed. And you will find Himself growing into your own life.

"God the Word," how we thank Thee for the revelation of Thyself to us. We are Thine. Thou art ours. Amen.

---

328. THAT ETERNAL LIFE

That eternal life, which was with the Father, and was manifested unto us.

1 JOHN 1:2

John says, "We have seen Him who is Life Eternal. We are witnesses to that fact and we want you to have the assurance that your joy may be full." And Paul says, "For in Him dwelleth all the fullness of the Godhead bodily." *He is* Eternal Life. He has imparted Eternal Life to us through the channel of faith and the indwelling Holy Spirit certifies to it. Nothing can ever separate us from the love of God which is in Christ Jesus our Lord. We are God's rich sons. Our treasures are for evermore. "Oh, happy day, that fixed our choice!" *Let us go out and tell it anywhere and everywhere.*

Oh, Blessed One, our Eternal Life, we wait for Thy coming. Come quickly. Amen.

329. THE ADVOCATE

My little children, these things write I unto you,
that ye sin not. And if any man sin, we have an
advocate with the Father, Jesus Christ the righteous.

1 JOHN 2:1

Sin is the existing nature of man. God, in love, has recognized the need of man and has made provision for that need. We sin when we "come short of the glory of God." So Christ becomes our *Advocate* or "One who comes alongside," which is the meaning of "advocate." He comes to stand by us. When Satan charges us with sin, Christ represents us and defends us. He is the Attorney who handles our case. His propitiation (or covering for sin) is manifested in all His work for us—in His life, His death, His resurrection, His ascension, and His intercession.

Lord, we thank Thee that Thou dost
appear for us and through Thee, we are
all accepted by our Heavenly Father. Amen.

---

330. JESUS CHRIST THE RIGHTEOUS

If any man sin, we have an advocate with
the Father, Jesus Christ the righteous.

1 JOHN 2:1

Jesus Christ is the Righteous One. "Righteous" means "right" or "just." There never was another perfectly righteous man, for the Scripture says, "There is none righteous; *no, not one.*" "All have sinned." No unrighteous man could be our Advocate or Judge. He must Himself be just, and He is, and He is also the Justifier (Romans 3:20). What a consolation to us as poor sinners to know that we are justified from all things from which we could not be justified by the law of Moses.

Lord Jesus, we pour out our hearts to Thee.
Thou hast settled forever what we could
never have settled. Hallelujah! Amen.

---

331. THE PROPITIATION

And he is the propitiation for our sins: and not for
ours only, but also for the sins of the whole world.
1 JOHN 2:2

The sin question is the great question. Sin separates us from God. His wrath against sin must be appeased, satisfied, and the provision for that satisfaction is in His Son (Romans 3:25): "Whom God hath set forth to be a propitiation through faith in his blood. . .through the forbearance of God." Wonderful love of God the Father; wonderful love of Jesus, His Son our Saviour; wonderful love of the Holy Spirit, the One who makes the fact of propitiation clear to us through the Word! How is the "whole world" to know this truth? Someone must go. Will *we* go?

Oh, Loving Lord, Thy love is wonderful. The price
Thou hast paid is wonderful. Help us today
to tell out the wonderful story. Amen.

332. THE SON

And we have seen and do testify that the Father
sent the Son to be the Saviour of the world.
1 JOHN 4:14

The apostle John is making full proof of his ministry. He is testifying to the truth from his own personal experience, conscious that he is indwelt by the Spirit and has the new nature. He says that the Son was sent for one specific purpose—to be the Saviour of men, lost men. The business of the believer is to testify to that fact. The greatest business in the world is to follow in the footsteps of men like John, the fisher of men. It is not a question of church membership or of worldly possessions, but of knowledge of Him. Have you seen Him? Do you know Him? Then go and testify of Him.

Son of God, Saviour of lost men, send us
out with Thy love message today. Amen.

---

333. THE SAVIOUR OF THE WORLD

And we have seen and do testify that the Father
sent the Son to be the Saviour of the world.
1 JOHN 4:14

A lost and ruined world, bound by the shackles of sin, dominated by the demon Satan, helpless and hopeless! What can be done? Only God, the Sovereign against whom the world has sinned, can solve the question, and He has. He sent His Son. We have seen Him by faith and testify to the truth that He is indeed a Saviour. He has saved us through faith in His name and finished work. We *must* testify. We *must* bear witness. Wherever we go, whatever we do, let us tell it out—"He is a world Saviour."

Lord, may we be faithful witnesses to Thy saving power and tell the love story to all. Amen.

---

334. THE TRUE GOD

And we know that the Son of God is come, and hath given us an understanding, that we may know him that is true, and we are in him that is true, even in his Son Jesus Christ. This is the true God, and eternal life.

1 JOHN 5:20

In His prayer on that last night, Jesus said to the Father: "As Thou hast given Him power over *all flesh* that He should give eternal life to as many as Thou hast given Him; and this is life eternal that they should know Thee, the only true God, and Jesus Christ whom Thou hast sent." Here it is made evident that "we are in Him that is true, even His Son Jesus Christ, the *true God* and eternal life." There is but *one* God. "Great is the mystery of godliness" but we praise God—*the True God*—that we are in Him and He in us. Nothing can ever separate us.

Lord Jesus, Thou who art the True God, help us to live out that great and glorious life that Thou hast imparted to us. Amen.

335. ETERNAL LIFE

This is the true God, and eternal life.

1 JOHN 5:20

Jesus is "the True God" and He is "*Eternal Life*" also. Human life is eternal, for it must be lived here or in another world. It must be spent in the heart of God our Saviour, or in the abode of Satan. "Where will you spend eternity?" is one of the most solemn questions ever asked of men. The only answer is found in God's Word, and it is answered there a hundred times and in a hundred ways. To believers, eternity means life with God our Saviour, and we look forward with joyful anticipation; but to the unsaved, it is a fearful prospect.

*Lord, help us in dealing with people to be
truthful and loving as we paint the pictures
of a future without a Saviour. Amen.*

---

336. THE SON OF THE FATHER

*Grace be with you, mercy, and peace, from God
the Father, and from the Lord Jesus Christ,
the Son of the Father, in truth and love.*

2 JOHN 3

Here is a three-fold blessing bestowed by John: "Grace, mercy and peace from the Son of the Father." This is the testimony of the Father: "This is My beloved Son in whom I am well pleased," and He is the *only begotten* of the Father. There is no separation between Father and

Son. There is a union which is unspeakable. "He that hath seen me hath seen the Father." "I and My Father are one." The blessing is to be bestowed in "truth and love." Truth without love may be cold, hard, harsh. Love without truth may be purely sentimental, but, when combined, they truly represent the message of "the Son of the Father," for the Son *is* the Truth, manifested in Love.

We pray, our Father, that this benediction of grace, mercy, and peace may rest upon us this day as we meditate upon "the Son of the Father." Amen.

337. JESUS CHRIST

Grace be unto you, and peace, from him which is, and which was, and which is to come; and from the seven Spirits which are before his throne; and from Jesus Christ, who is the faithful witness, and the first begotten of the dead, and the prince of the kings of the earth.

REVELATION 1:4–5

Here is a four-fold adoration of our Lord. Four titles are given Him, the first of which is "*Jesus Christ*" (the Anointed Saviour). "How sweet the name of Jesus sounds to a believer's ear." He is, He was, and He is to come! That completes the vision of Himself. The "seven spirits before the Throne" represent the seven-fold operation of the Lord throughout the earth. We must join with the Heavenly host and sing His praises.

Oh, Thou anointed Saviour, help us to unite with all the
Heavenly host in glorifying Thy name. Amen.

---

338. THE FAITHFUL WITNESS

Jesus Christ, who is the faithful witness.
REVELATION 1:5

This was the testimony of Christ Himself when He
stood before Pilate (John 18:37): "To this end was I born
and for this cause came I unto the world, that I should
bear witness unto the truth. Everyone that is of the
truth heareth my voice." This was His mission—to bear
faithful witness. This is the obligation of every believer,
"Ye shall be witnesses of Me." This is the failure in a large
measure of the church. The unsaved are waiting for the
testimony by lip and life of professing Christians, and
as they behold it, they are convicted by the Holy Spirit.

May the Holy Spirit Himself so control our lives
that we shall count it our highest privilege to
manifest Him before a gainsaying world. Amen.

---

339. THE FIRST BEGOTTEN
OF THE DEAD

Jesus Christ, who is. . .the first begotten of the dead.
REVELATION 1:5

Jesus Christ raised Lazarus from the dead, but He
Himself came forth from the grave by His own power.

Lazarus died again, but Jesus Christ "ever liveth to make intercession for us." He was the first-born of the dead. He is the forerunner of the saints who shall also be raised from the dead. "But now is Christ risen from the dead and become the first-fruits of them that slept." "We know that when He shall appear, we shall be like Him for we shall see Him as He is." "Who shall change our vile body that it may be fashioned like unto His glorious body."

Our Lord, we look and long for Thy coming
in Thy glorified body that we may be
with Thee and like Thee. Amen.

340. THE PRINCE OF THE KINGS OF THE EARTH

Jesus Christ, who is. . .the prince of the kings of the earth.
REVELATION 1:5

A glorious title! Some-time in the future there will be a gathering of all the hosts that have ever lived on this earth, and of the hosts of Heaven, and in their presence will stand *One* who will be proclaimed "Prince of the kings of the earth—King of kings and Lord of lords!" The kingdoms of the world are His by right and title, and before Him all must bow. He is Lord of all who exercise authority and King of all who reign. He has not yet asserted His authoritative rights. They are still in abeyance but the day is coming when every sceptre will be broken and every crown laid at His feet.

We praise Thee, Lord of Hosts, our Saviour;
we will be with Thee then. Help us to do
our best to hasten the glad day. Amen.

---

341. THE ALPHA AND OMEGA

I am Alpha and Omega, the beginning and the
ending, saith the Lord, which is, and which
was, and which is to come, the Almighty.
REVELATION 1:8

"Alpha" is the first letter of the Greek alphabet, and
"Omega" is the last. So our Lord is First and Last. He
is the Source of all things. He is the Source of all truth,
of all the promises given in the Word of God, of all the
prophecies, of all commands and of all penalties. How
great is our Lord, "which is and which was and which is
to come"—the All-inclusive One! Everything is involved
in the two words, "beginning" and "ending," and one
word includes it all—"Is."

Oh, Thou Jehovah-Elohim, First and Last, who seest
and knowest all things, hold us by Thy hand. Amen.

---

342. THE ALMIGHTY

I am. . .the Almighty.
REVELATION 1:8

Our Lord Jesus Christ is the All-sufficient One. Listen
to His voice—the "I Am" speaking to us. His voice and

message demand attention and obedience. We can trust Him and trust His message. Nothing can fail of all that He says. The Bible is an infallible book. Its message is an infallible message and it says: "I will receive you and will be a Father unto you, and ye shall be my sons and daughters, saith the Lord Almighty" (2 Corinthians 6:17–18). And again, "He that dwelleth in the secret place of the Most High shall abide under the shadow of the Almighty" (Psalm 91:1). What an abiding place for us who are His dear children!

Oh, Thou Almighty One, we submit to Thee
today, and to Thine All-power. Help us
to dwell with and in Thee. Amen.

343. THE FIRST AND THE LAST

And he laid his right hand upon me, saying unto me,
Fear not; I am the first and the last.
REVELATION 1:17

He was the First-begotten. He said of Himself, "Before Abraham was, I am." And John the Baptist said, "He was before me." "In the beginning was the Word and the Word was with God, and the Word was God; the same was in the beginning with God." He puts His right hand on us, that hand of power, and says in tenderest tones, "Fear not." He draws us to Himself with that same hand and says, "Pillow your head upon My shoulder. Have no fear. You are Mine. I purchased you at a great price. Perfect love casts out fear." He was *First* in His love for us when we were in sin. He is the *Last One* to forget or forsake us.

> *Blessed Lord, may we have that perfect*
> *love which casteth out all fear. Amen.*

---

344. HE THAT LIVETH

> *I am he that liveth, and was dead;*
> *and, behold, I am alive for evermore, Amen.*
> REVELATION 1:18

He liveth and abideth forever. He ever liveth to make intercession for us. In love for us and through grace He died for us. He bowed His head and gave up His Spirit. The bars of death were broken. He tore them away. He is living now and will live to the ages of ages, and He holds the keys of death and hell (or Hades). "He has the keys"—the complete mastery. He has the right to open and shut. Binding and loosing are at His command. The sting of death is sin and the strength of sin is the law, but thanks be to God who giveth us the victory through our Lord Jesus Christ! Praise be to Thy name, thou Victor over death!

> *We await Thy coming and the*
> *shout from Heaven. Amen.*

345. THE MORNING STAR

And I will give him the morning star.
Revelation 2:28

He will give us Himself, for He is the Morning Star.
Again, we hear the voice of the Holy Spirit coming with
a heart message for the beloved of the Lord. We are bone
of His bone and flesh of His flesh. The stars are for the
night, and it is night now for this poor old world that lieth
in the lap of the Wicked One. It grows darker and darker
and midnight is upon us, but our eyes are Heavenward.
We hear His promise. As the "Sun of Righteousness" to
Israel He brought them blessings; but before the glad day
for Israel comes, the Morning Star must shine, and a ray
of light will appear for His own Heavenly ones.

Lord, keep us close to Thyself. Keep us loyal.
Keep our eyes upon the skies as we labor
for Thee and for Thy coming. Amen.

---

346. THE HIDDEN MANNA

To him that overcometh will I
give to eat of the hidden manna.
Revelation 2:17

What is this Hidden Manna? Is it not Himself who is
the Bread of Life? The voice of the Holy Spirit is heard
speaking to the churches a message for the overcomers.
Food awaits them. For twelve thousand and five hundred
days manna was rained down from Heaven for the

children of Israel. From the glory land our Lord feeds His flock with the Word of God—the Word made flesh. We who feed upon Him shall live forever. We have the white stone and the new name.

Thou art speaking to us, our Lord. We hear. We await the day and the new name which Thou wilt give to us. Amen.

---

347. THE AMEN

These things saith the Amen.
REVELATION 3:14

"Amen" is "So be it" or "So it is." The "Amen" here is our Lord—the Faithful Witness. He has said "Amen" to every truth of the Scripture, but the church has failed to follow in His footsteps. She has the truth for she has Himself, and He is the Way, the Truth and the Life, as we have seen; but she has not said "Amen." She says, "I am rich and increased with goods and have need of nothing." She has not been a faithful and true witness. She has been neither cold nor hot, but a lukewarm product. God pity her! To what extent are we responsible? God forgive us. God help us.

Lord, open our eyes to see, our ears to hear, and our hearts to believe. Baptize us with the power of the Holy Spirit. Amen.

348. THE FAITHFUL
AND TRUE WITNESS

These things saith. . .the faithful and true witness.
REVELATION 3:14

We have viewed Him as the Faithful Witness, but He is
also the Faithful and *True* Witness. Is it not wonderful?
How marvellously the Holy Spirit emphasizes the
character of Christ for us. Here we have the "Amen"
amplified. The word "faithful" asserts the truthfulness
of "True" for it implies "real and complete." He had
seen that which He attested, and He was competent
and willing to faithfully witness. Has the church been
a faithful and true witness? No, she has not. Let us
come a little closer. Have *we* been faithful and true
witnesses? Alas, we must bow our heads with shame as
we remember our failure. Will we be?

Oh, Lord our Saviour, forgive us for our faithlessness
as witnesses. Anoint us to stand before a lost
world and be TRUE at any cost. Amen.

---

349. THE BEGINNING OF
THE CREATION OF GOD

These things saith. . .the beginning of the creation of God.
REVELATION 3:14

There are four headships ascribed to our Lord Jesus Christ.
First—of the body: "Head over all things to the church,
which is his body" (Ephesians 1:22–23). Second—of the

race: "Ye are all one in Christ Jesus" (Galatians 3:28). Third—of the creation: "Who is the image of the invisible God, the first born of every creature" (Colossians 1:15). Fourth—of every man: "But I would have you know that the head of every man is Christ" (1 Corinthians 11:3). Let us seek earnestly to recognize the might and power and authority of our Lord who left Heaven and laid down His life for us.

Oh, Thou Mighty One, creator of all things, help us to recognize Thee today and to love and serve Thee. Amen.

---

350. THE LION OF THE TRIBE OF JUDAH

Behold, the Lion of the tribe of Judah. . .hath prevailed to open the book, and to loose the seven seals thereof.
REVELATION 5:5

The dying prophecy of Jacob was fulfilled in Jesus: "The sceptre shall not depart from Judah, nor a law-giver from between His feet until Shiloh come" (Genesis 49:10). Judah had no conception that nearly three thousand years would pass before his prophecy would or could be fulfilled, or that its fulfillment would involve the glorified Son of God. The characteristics of a lion are manifest in the life and work of the Messiah. He will arrest every opposing force of Satan and establish His universal kingdom. Glory be to God, we will be with Him and like Him in the final overthrow of Satan's kingdom.

Lord, help us to be like Thee now. Help us to wear the
armor of warriors and carry the Sword of the Spirit. Amen.

---

351. THE ROOT OF DAVID

Weep not: behold, the Lion of the tribe of
Judah, the Root of David, hath prevailed.
REVELATION 5:5

King David was the representative of *Royalty*; Moses of
the *Law*; Abraham of the *Promises*. Here, Christ is seen
in relation to His throne and kingdom rights. "A Root"
from the stem, or branch of David (Isaiah 11:1). "And
there shall come forth a rod out of the stem of Jesse, and
a Branch shall grow out of his roots." Jesus was the Root
that was to rise and reign over the Gentiles and in Him
would the Gentiles trust. He was worthy to open the
book because He was slain. What wonders confront us
concerning Him!

Lord, we marvel more and more that Thou couldst ever
love us and die for us, Thou who art the Mighty One.
But we bow at Thy feet in worship and praise. Amen.

---

352. HOLY AND TRUE

How long, O Lord, holy and true, dost thou not judge
and avenge our blood on them that dwell on the earth?
REVELATION 6:10

This is the heart cry of those who suffered death for Jesus'
sake because they were true to Him in life and testimony.

Is it not such a cry as sometimes bursts forth from our own souls as we see the hellish hatred of Satan for the souls of men? "How long, O Lord, how long, Thou Holy and True One?" But we must abide in faith. He says, "What I do thou knowest not now but thou shalt know hereafter." How marvellous is the grace and patience of God our Saviour! But the day is coming when the Righteous Judge will render His judgment.

Thou Holy and True One, we look to Thee in full assurance of faith. Keep us close to Thyself this day. Amen.

---

353. THE LAMB IN THE MIDST OF THE THRONE

For the Lamb which is in the midst of the throne shall feed them, and shall lead them unto living fountains of waters: and God shall wipe away all tears from their eyes.
REVELATION 7:17

Here is a wonderful picture of our future dwelling place. We are before the throne of God. Our robes have been made white in the blood of the Lamb. We shall not know hunger or thirst any more. He that sitteth upon the throne will dwell amongst us. No more hunger or thirst for us. He, Himself, shall feed us and we shall drink from the living fountains. Tears will be wiped away forever. What has made all this possible? *One Thing*—the blood! *One Person*—the Lamb! We shall dwell through eternity with Him, be with Him and like Him.

Wonderful Lord and wonderful Love, help us
to dwell ever in Thy presence and feed us
with the Heavenly manna now. Amen.

---

354. THE LAMB SLAIN

And all that dwell upon the earth shall worship him,
whose names are not written in the book of life of
the Lamb slain from the foundation of the world.
REVELATION 13:8

Jesus was ordained from the foundation of the world to suffer upon the cross for our sins. The death of Christ has been efficacious to put away sin, from the beginning. The only means of salvation for men has been the shedding of His blood. That was foreknown and foreordained of God. What a place in our hearts should the Lamb of God have! What a place should the blood of Christ have, by which we are redeemed! For "without the shedding of blood there is no remission."

Blessed Lamb of God, we adore Thee. We praise Thy name.
We rejoice that we are washed in Thy blood. Amen.

---

355. KING OF SAINTS

Just and true are thy ways, thou King of saints.
REVELATION 15:3

This title is better rendered "King of Nations" or "King of the Ages." What a picture is here! We are standing by the glassy sea, mingled with fire. A judgment is awaiting the nations. Seven angels with the seven last plagues are there. Mark seems to describe this time: "For in those days shall be affliction, such as was not from the beginning of the creation which God created, unto this time, neither shall be" (Mark 13:19). But there are the harps of God and the song of Moses. The song is of victory over the beast and his image. What a day! What joy for our adored Lord!

We want to pledge to Thee, today, our loyal devotion,
Thou King of Nations. Help us to do Thy Holy
Will until the coming of "the day." Amen.

---

356. LORD OF LORDS

For he is Lord of lords, and King of kings: and they
that are with him are called, and chosen, and faithful.
REVELATION 17:14

From the story of the Garden of Eden until the scene described in this verse, the powers of earth and hell have fought against our Lord. The prince of this world and the prince of the power of the air has shown his Satanic hatred for Christ, who is the Promised One and who will bruise his head. The world has been the sphere of the conflict of the ages, but, thanks be to God, there is coming a day when that war will cease and that is the day which is portrayed in this verse. All of the kings must bow to Him. It has been an age-long conflict but the end must come. We look forward to the victory which is prophesied.

Thou, who dost hold the worlds in the hollow of Thy hand,
hasten the glad, victorious day of Thy coming. Amen.

---

357. KING OF KINGS

The Lamb shall overcome them:
for he is. . .King of kings.
REVELATION 17:14

He has upon His garments and upon His thigh the name
"King of kings." Who has? The One who was born in
a manger and who fellowshipped with fishermen as He
longs to fellowship with us today. A sharp sword issues
from His mouth—the Sword of the Spirit, which is the
Word of God. As His enemies fell before His presence in
the Garden, so fall they then. The power of God's Word
is *irresistible*. How foolish are they whose feeble hands are
raised up against the King of kings—the Mighty One!
What judgment awaits all those who oppose Him and
His unerring Word.

King of kings, we bow to Thee. We follow Thee.
Help us to fight the good fight of faith. Amen.

---

358. LORD GOD OMNIPOTENT

And I heard as it were the voice of a great multitude,
and as the voice of many waters, and as the
voice of mighty thunderings, saying, Alleluia:
for the Lord God omnipotent reigneth.
REVELATION 19:6

Here is a climax. What words can compare with the words of God which are associated with this matchless scene: "And after these things I heard a great voice of much people in Heaven, saying, Alleluia; Salvation, and glory, and honor, and power, unto the Lord our God. . . . Let us be glad and rejoice and give honor to Him; for the marriage of the Lamb is come and His wife hath made herself ready." The time is not far distant. He is coming, the Omnipotent One—and we will be with Him. Alleluia!

Oh, Thou Mighty One, gird us with Thy strength, that we may do our best to hasten that glad day. Amen.

---

359. FAITHFUL AND TRUE

And he that sat upon him was called Faithful and True.
REVELATION 19:11

To no one else could that title be applied but the Lord Jesus, who was Himself the Way, the Truth and the Life. He was faithful to the truth always and faithful in its application, whether in promises of blessings or cursing. Listen to the precious promise, "I will come again and receive you unto Myself that where I am, there ye may be also." But the other is equally true, "Depart from Me, ye workers of iniquity. There shall be weeping and wailing and gnashing of teeth." There is no change in Him, the Living Word, and not one jot or tittle can be changed in the Written Word.

Lord, we believe in Thee and in Thy Word. May we never depart from it. Keep us faithful and true to Thee until the long expected call comes and we shall be taken up to be with Thee forever. Amen.

---

360. WORD OF GOD

And he was clothed with a vesture dipped in blood: and his name is called The Word of God.

REVELATION 19:13

How can we attempt to embody in a few words what this title demands? John only uses the term. John says, "without him was not anything made that was made. . . . And the Word was made flesh." How glad we are that we have heard His Word. We have seen Him by faith. He dwells in us and among us. Clothed in a blood-dipped vesture, He leads the armies of Heaven, including all the saints of the Old and New Testament, to victory. Pity those whose eyes have been closed to the vision of the real Christ and who only have a sentimental conception of Him.

We bow at Thy feet, blessed Word of God, and lift our voices as we sing, "Hallelujah! What a Saviour!" Amen.

361. THE TEMPLE

And I saw no temple therein: for the Lord God
Almighty and the Lamb are the temple of it.
REVELATION 21:22

What a wonderful Temple! He is the Temple! The city is four-square, as was the Holy of Holies; twelve thousand furlongs—fifteen hundred square miles! Whatever significance there may be in the dimensions and the structure—whether literal or pictorial—it means, "Great in size; rich in adornment." The city is of pure gold, like clear glass; walls of jasper, upon that sapphire, then chalcedony, emerald, sardonyx, sardius, beryl, topaz, chrysoprasus, jacinth, amethyst; gates of one pearl; streets of gold. We stand in awe, but—glory be to God—we anticipate with increasing joy the vision which awaits us and its full realization.

Blessed One, keep us close to Thee with open ears
and open eyes, as we await the realization
of our fond anticipation. Amen.

---

362. THE LIGHT OF THE CITY

And the Lamb is the light thereof.
REVELATION 21:23

The Lamb is the "Light of the World" and He is also the Light of the Eternal, Four-square City. There is no need of sun or moon, for He who created all things hath provided a Light for the City and it is the glory of His own countenance—the Lamb of God who died upon the cross; the One who bore our sins and washed us in His own blood. By this Light the nations shall walk and in this Light kings and people will pay their tribute. We will be there. Hallelujah!

Lamb of God, Light of the World, we bask in
the sunshine of Thy love now and will in
the light of Thy glory hereafter. Amen.

---

363. THE OFFSPRING OF DAVID

I am the root and the offspring of David,
and the bright and morning star.
REVELATION 22:16

Christ is the Stem which sprang from the root of Jesse, and He is the Offspring of David. God, the Son, created the heavens and the earth and all that are therein, yet He is the Offspring of David, David's Lord, and David's Son. He was *born* King of the Jews and *died* King of the Jews and some day He will *reign* King of the Jews. This was God's promise and all of God's promises shall be fulfilled. As the Divine Creator, He is the Root of David's house; as Man, He is the Offspring. He sends His angel to give this testimony to us and to the world. There is no contradiction in God's Word concerning God's Son.

We glorify Thy Word and Thy work, our Lord.
We look into Thy face and adore Thee. Amen.

364. THE BRIGHT AND MORNING STAR

I Jesus have sent mine angel to testify unto you these things in the churches. I am. . .the bright and morning star.
REVELATION 22:16

We have meditated upon Christ as the "Day Star" and the "Morning Star," but here He, who is the Light of the World, speaks of Himself as the "Bright and Morning Star." Before the rising of the sun, before the millennium dawns, He will be to the church the "Bright and Morning Star." He will dispel the darkness for us before the prophesied judgments come upon a weary, sin-sick world; and before the glories depicted in this chapter are revealed, He will appear as the Bright and Morning Star. We must never cease to cherish this great truth, keeping our eyes fixed and our hopes centered upon Himself.

Lord, we are looking for the effulgent glory of Thy presence, Thou Bright and Morning Star. Amen.

---

365. THE TESTIFIER

He which testifieth these things saith, Surely I come quickly. Amen. Even so, come, Lord Jesus.
REVELATION 22:20

This is not a title, nor a name, but a fitting truth with which to close this little volume. We would rejoice if every reader has a heart-felt desire to say "Amen" to this promise of our Lord. The days grow darker for the church and for the world. The signs multiply as we look carefully at the prophecies. The poor old world reels like a drunken man to its doom. Our hearts are sad. We are thinking of those whose future is to be full of woe and anguish. "The Testifier" entreats us to go and testify to the lost. Let us point them to the Lamb of God and plead with sinners to accept Him and with the saints to look for Him. He has left *the Testimony*. And now, in closing, the last verse of this chapter is our heartfelt prayer for our readers:

"The grace of our Lord Jesus Christ be with you all." Amen.

SCRIPTURE INDEX

Regular type indicates pull-out verses
preceding devotional entries. Italics indicate
verses quoted or alluded to within the
devotional text. Numbers provided refer to
the entries rather than the page numbers.

GENESIS

1:3. . . . . *179*
1:3–4. . . . . *194*
3:15. 1
8:21. . . . . *257*
14 . . . . *297*
14:18–20. . . . . *294*
22:15. 2
49:10. . . . . .3, *350*
49:24. 4

EXODUS

3:5. . . . . *32*
16:31. 5
33:18, 19. . . . . *283*

LEVITICUS

2:1. 6
3:1. 7

NUMBERS

24:17. . . . . .8, 9

DEUTERONOMY
18:18. . . . .*188*

JOSHUA
5:14. 10

2 SAMUEL
22:47. 11
23:4. . . . . .12, 13

JOB
9:3. 14

PSALMS
3:3. . . . . .15, 16
9:10. . . . .*36*
18:2. 17
22:6. 18
23:1. 19
23:3. 20
24:8. . . . . .21, 22
24:10. 23
28:7. . . . .*156*
31:2. 24
31:3. 25
34:7. . . . .*311*
37:39. . . . .*156*
61:2. 26
61:3. 27
69:8. 28
72:1. 29

72:6. . . . . 30, 31
81:10. . . . . *121*
89:27. 32
90:17. . . . . *78*
91:1. . . . . *342*
92:10. . . . . *156*
107:9. . . . . *191*
118:14. . . . . *156*
118:22. 33
132:11. . . . . *154*
144:2. 34
148:13. 36

PROVERBS

8:12. 35
8:14. 37
18:24. 38
29:25. . . . . *311*

SONG OF SOLOMON

1:3. 39
1:13. 40
1:14. 41
2:1. . . . . 42, 43
3:2. 44
5:10. 45
5:16. 46

ISAIAH

4:2. 47
6:3. 48

7:14. . . . . *129*

7:16. 49

8:14. 50

9:2. 51

9:6. . . . . 52, 53, 54, 55, 56

10:17. 57

11:1. . . . . 58, 59, *351*

11:10. . . . . 60, 61

12:2. 62

22:23. . . . . 63, 64

25:4. . . . . 65, 66, 67

26:3. . . . . *208*

26:4. 68

28:5. . . . . 69, 70

28:16. . . . . 71, 72, 73

30:21. . . . . *203*

32:2. . . . . 74, 75, 76, 77

33:17. 78

33:22. 79

40:3. 80

40:10. 81

40:28. 82

42:1. 84

42:6. 83

49:2. 85

49:7. 86

52:13, 14. . . . . *258*

53:2. 87

53:2, 4. . . . . *58*

53:3. 88

53:5. . . . . *11*

53:7. . . . . *18*
53:11. 89
54:5. . . . . .90, 91
55:4. . . . . .92, 93, 94
59:16. . . . . *300*
59:20. 95
60:1. . . . . *158, 194*
60:20. 96
61:1–3. . . . . *168*
63:9. 97
64:8. 98

JEREMIAH
8:22. . . . . .99, 100
10:16. 101
14:8. 102
23:5. 103
29:13. . . . . *45*
30:9. 104
31:33–34. . . . . *304*
32:17. . . . . *54*
45:5. . . . . *322*
50:6. 105

EZEKIEL
18:4, 20. . . . . *305*
34:23. . . . . .106, 107
34:29. 108

DANIEL
2:34–35. 109

7:13–14. 110
8:25. 111

JOEL
3:16. 112

MICAH
5:2. 113

NAHUM
1:7. 114

ZECHARIAH
2:5. 115
3:8. 116
6:12. 118
9:9. . . . .*140*
14:4–5, 9. 117
14:5. 119
14:16. 120

MALACHI
3:1. 121
3:3. . . . . .122, 123
4:2. 124

MATTHEW
1:1. . . . . .125, 126, 127
1:21. 128
1:23. 129
2:6. 130

2:9. 131
2:23. 132
3:17. . . . .*139*
4:16. . . . .*164*
5:8. . . . .*48, 78*
5:17, 18. . . . .*204*
11:19. 133
11:28. . . . .*105, 275*
12:18. . . . . .134, 135
13:37. 136
16:16. 137
16:20. 138
17:5. 139
18:3. . . . .*49*
19:17. . . . .*148*
21:11. 140
23:8. 141
25:10. 142
27:25. . . . .*321*
28:19–20. . . . .*129*

MARK

1:24. 143
1:34. . . . .*143*
3:31, 34. . . . .*144*
3:35. 144
5:7. . . . . .145, *154*
6:3. . . . . .146, 147
6:34. . . . .*313*
9:31. . . . .*149*
10:17. 148

10:33.	149
10:45.	150
12:6.	151
12:37.	*184*
13:19.	*355*
14:61.	152
15:2.	153
16:15.	*242*

LUKE

1:26–28.	*132*
1:32.	154
1:47.	155
1:69.	156
1:76.	157
1:78.	158
2:11.	159
2:12.	160
2:25.	161
2:26.	162
2:30.	163
2:32.	164, 165
2:34.	166
2:43.	167
2:49.	*87, 167*
4:23.	168
6:5.	169
6:40.	*141*
7:16.	170
9:20.	171
10:33.	172

13:25. 173
19:7. 174
19:12. 175
19:13. . . . .*167*
23:35. 176
23:46. . . . .*219*
24:19. 177
24:39. . . . .*327*

JOHN
1:1. . . . . .178, *343*
1:1–2. . . . .*327*
1:3. . . . .*269*
1:3, 14. . . . .*360*
1:4. . . . .*83*, 179
1:9. 180
1:14. 181
1:18. . . . .*284*
1:29. 182
1:34. 183
1:49. . . . . .184, 185
1:51. . . . .*185*
3:16. 186
4:10. 187
4:25. 188
4:42. 189
5:22. . . . .*307*
6:32. 190
6:33. 191
6:35. 192
6:51. 193

7:37. . . . .*77*
7:46. . . . .*234*
8:12. 194
8:58. 195
10:4. . . . .*35*
10:7. 196
10:9. . . . .*196, 286*
10:11. 197
10:16. 198
10:18. . . . .*255*
10:30. . . . .*259, 336*
11:25. 199
11:27. 200
12:23–24. 201
12:28. . . . .*139*
13:7. . . . .*352*
13:13. 202
14:6. . . . . .203, 204, 205
14:9. . . . .*92, 336*
14:19. . . . .*78*
14:21. . . . .*79*
14:27. . . . .*56, 252, 271, 298*
15 . . . .*47*
15:5. 206
15:7. . . . .*47*
15:13. . . . .*135, 255*
16:8, 10. . . . .*124*
16:13–14. . . . .*141*
16:23. . . . .*228*
16:28. . . . .*273*
16:33. 207

17:2–3. . . . . *334*
17:12. 208
17:18. 209
17:20. . . . . *209*
18:37. . . . . *338*
19:5. 210
20:28. 211

ACTS
1:8. . . . . *338*
1:11. . . . . *280*
2:22. 212
2:27. 213
3:14. 214
3:15. 215
4:12. . . . . *314*
4:27. 216
5:31. 217
7:52. 218
7:59. 219
10:36. 220
10:42. 221
10:44. . . . . *220*
13:2. . . . . *281*
17:31. 222
22:8. 223

ROMANS
3:10. . . . . *124, 330*
3:20. . . . . *330*
3:23. . . . . *329, 330*

3:25.	*331*
5:8.	*135*
5:12.	*305*
5:21.	224
8:29.	225
8:32.	226, *248*
9:5.	227
10:4.	*297*
10:12.	228
10:13.	229
10:15, 17.	*229*
11:26.	230
14:9.	231
14:11.	*108*
15:8.	232

1 CORINTHIANS

1:24.	233, 234
1:30.	235, 236, 237
2:8.	238
3:9.	*292*
3:11.	239
3:12.	*25, 278*
3:19.	*234*
3:21–23.	*101*
5:7.	240
10:4.	241
10:13.	*67*
11:3.	242, *349*
11:30.	*193*
15:10.	*90*
15:20.	243, *266, 339*
15:45.	244, 246

15:47. 245
15:56–57. . . . .*344*
15:58. . . . .*89*

2 CORINTHIANS
4:4. 247
6:17–18. . . . .*342*
9:15. 248

GALATIANS
3:9. . . . .*127*
3:28. . . . .*349*

EPHESIANS
1:3. 249
1:22. 250
1:22–23. . . . .*349*
1:23. 251
2:14. 252
2:14–15. . . . .*298*
2:22. . . . .*239*
3:8–9. . . . .*263*
3:20. . . . .*168*
4:5. 253
4:15. 254
5:2. . . . . .255, 256, 257

PHILIPPIANS
1:21. . . . .*268*
2:7. 258
2:8. . . . .*323*
2:9. . . . .*1, 314*
3:21. . . . .*339*
4:6. . . . .*3*

COLOSSIANS

1:2. 259
1:13. 260
1:15. . . . . 261, 262, *349*
1:16. 263
1:18. . . . . 264, 265, 266
1:27. 267
3:4. 268
3:11. 269
3:24. . . . . 270, *307*

1 THESSALONIANS

1:5. . . . .*161*
4:16. . . . .*243*
4:17. . . . . *12, 63*

2 THESSALONIANS

3:16. 271

1 TIMOTHY

1:1. . . . . 272, *281*
1:15. 273
2:5. . . . . 274, 275
3:16. 276
6:15. 277

2 TIMOTHY

4:1–2. 278
4:7. . . . .*89*
4:8. 279

TITUS

2:13. 280
3:4. 281

HEBREWS

1:2. 282
1:3. .283, 284, 285, 286
1:8. 287
2:10. 288
2:16. 289
3:1. . . . . .290, 291
3:3. 292
4:14. 293
4:15. . . . .*87*
5:6. 294
5:9. 295
6:20. 296
7:2. . . . . .297, 298
7:22. 299
7:25. . . . . .300, *339*
7:26. . . . . .301, 302
8:2. 303
8:6. 304
9:16. 305
9:22. . . . .*354*
10:16. . . . .*121*
10:37. 306
11:6. 307
12:2. . . . . .308, 309
12:24. 310
13:5. 311

13:6. 311
13:8. . . . . *52*, *126*, 312
13:20. 313
13:21. . . . .*313*

JAMES
1:2. . . . .*308*
1:5–6. . . . .*234*
2:7. 314
5:14. . . . .*100*

1 PETER
1:19. 315
2:4. *176*, 317, *319*
2:6. 316, 318, 319
2:7. . . . .*319*
2:7–8. . . . . 320, 321
2:21. . . . .*73*
2:25. 322
3:18. 323
5:4. 324

2 PETER
1:4. . . . .*5*
1:19. 325
2:24. . . . .*11*
3:18. 326

1 JOHN
1:1. 327
1:2. 328

1:5. . . . . *51, 194*
2:1. . . . . 329, 330
2:2. 331
3:2. . . . .*339*
3:3. . . . .*70*
4:14. . . . . .332, 333
5:12. . . . .*246*
5:20. . . . . .334, 335

2 JOHN
3 336

REVELATION
1:4–5. 337
1:5. . . . . 338, 339, 340
1:6. . . . .*294*
1:8. . . . . .341, 342
1:14. . . . .*110*
1:15. . . . .*85*
1:17. 343
1:18. 344
2:17. 346
2:28. 345
3:12. . . . .*63, 72*
3:14. 347, 348, 349
4:2–3. . . . .*64*
5:5. . . . . .350, 351
6:10. 352
6:15–16. . . . .*321*
7:17. 353
13:8. 354

15:3. 355
17:14. . . . . .356, 357
19:1, 7. . . . .*358*
19:6. 358
19:9. . . . .*142*
19:11. 359
19:13. 360
21:22. 361
21:23. 362
22:12. . . . .*307*
22:16. . . . . .363, 364
22:20. 365